Karate-do

THE WAY OF Shito-ryu

By

DEL SAITO

REVISED EDITION

AWP LLC/Empire Books
Los Angeles, CA

DISCLAIMER:

Please note that the author and publisher of this book are NOT RESPONSIBLE in any manner whatsoever for any injury that may result from practicing the techniques and/or following the instructions given within. Since the physical activities described herein may be too strenuous in nature for some readers to engage in safely, it is essential that a physician be consulted prior to training.

Revised Edition First publish in 2023 by AWP LLC/Empire Books.

EMPIRE BOOKS
P.O. BOX 491788
LOS ANGELES, CA 90049

First edition; Library of Congress Catalog Number: ISBN-13: 978-1-949753-56-1

23 22 21 20 19 18 17 16 15 14 13 12

Library of Congress Cataloging-in-Publication Data:

Shito ryu karate / by Del Saito.—1st revised ed. p. cm. Includes index.
ISBN 978-1-949753-56-1 (pbk.: alk. paper) 1. Karate. 5. Martial arts–technique.
3. Large type books. I. Title. GV1222.3.F715 20146069.715'3–dc24
2006013287.

DEDICATION

I wish to dedicate this book to my parents, Toshio and Clara Saito, for their never ending love and support; to John and Carmen Isabelo for their many years of friendship and guidance; to my first instructor Al Kahalekulu, who kick-started my Karate journey; to Kenzo Mabuni, my seito Shito-ryu Karate-do sensei, who trusted me to carry on his Shito-ryu Karate-do legacy; to Tsukasa Mabuni (Miwako), the present headmaster of Seito Shito-ryu; and to Hiroko Mabuni, dedicated wife of Kenzo Mabuni.

Al Kahalekulu

Toshio & Clara Saito   *Carmen & John Isabelo*

Kenzo Mabuni   *Hiroko and Tsukasa Mabuni*

"The ultimate aim of Karate lies not in victory nor defeat, but in the perfection of the character of its participants." - Gichin Funakoshi

ACKNOWLEDGMENTS

Much appreciation goes to my friend Jose Fraguas who came up with the suggestion to restore this book from its original publication.

I would like to thank the many students and instructors who kindly gave their time to pose for the demonstration photographs in this book.

I appreciate all the numerous photos taken by our photographers Jerred Shoemaker, Steve Monroe, Chuck Aoto, and Mike Rodriguez.

Thanks also to Debbie Illingworth, Paul Bunch, and Ron Gandee-for their assistance in the production of this book, and to the staff at Empire Books.

To Christine Crawford, owner of Precision Printing, for her help in printing copies of this book for editing.

Many thanks to Janie Burstein for taking the time to help me edit this book.

I am also grateful to all my Shihan Kai members, International affiliated directors, instructors, and students who let me take a little from their lives in order to extend mine.

Jose Fraguas, author of "Shito-ryu Masters" and editor for "Masters Magazine."

The Karate forms that are practiced represents the art and culture of a style.

PREFACE

Welcome to the Karate-do world. The training program that you have chosen will bring added enjoyment, better health, and increased meaning to your life.

You have probably decided to try Karate for one or more of the following reasons: self-defense, physical conditioning, sport, confidence, self-discipline, to tap inner resources, or just plain curiosity. Whatever your reason, rest assured that you will receive the finest Karate-do instruction one could possibly ask for.

Our course involves professionally prepared exercises, techniques, and programs of Karate based on many years of dedication and Karate experience. It assures steady, thorough progress toward the goals you desire. Everything required for maximum knowledge, proficiency, and skill has been designed so that you follow each fundamental step with the next logical step. Because our training program is standardized, you can move from one branch to another, or from one instructor to another, without retracing your steps or slowing the learning progress.

This book begins with a brief discussion of the history and philosophy of Karate-do. It also contains important and informative materials necessary to help you understand and remember each area of your Karate training.

The meaningful things in life come through hard work, discipline, dedication, and effort. So it is with Karate-do. It is my sincere wish that you will train with an open mind and search earnestly for the true way of Karate. And that someday soon, you too will make Karate-do a meaningful part of your life.

I have taken the liberty to edit the original manuscript both in text and photographs, for better clarity, and hopefully enjoyment to all readers.

- Del Saito

FOREWORD

I am grateful to Jose Fraguas sensei for restoring this book on Shito-ryu Karate-do. Initially, I wrote this book as groundwork for Karate enthusiasts who were interested in Shito-ryu, primarily members of the International Karate Federation. This work was to be mandatory reading for all IKF members, so my hope was to educate them in the basic principles of Karate.

This work turned out to be a mixed blessing. I was able to share my knowledge of Karate, increasing awareness and interest for those that read the book searching for a deeper understanding. On the other hand, the acceptance of my ethical views shared in the book, those which I find integral to the practice of Karate, were dismissed and therefore the book was not accepted as viable mandatory reading. I have always placed honor before all else in my life, and the important lessons engrained in me by my parents since childhood were always the cornerstone of my Karate practice and teachings. It is my observation that many martial arts instructors do not follow or teach a strict code of ethics, and in worse case scenarios will run their dojos in a manner which simply enhances their egos. Karate-do, the way of Karate, should be a means to embrace honor with strong moral, social, and philosophical teachings, demonstrated by the instructor's example.

Many modern Karate schools have emerged whose teachings revolve solely on sport competition. As a result, students in today's schools never find the real treasure of Karate. Since I appreciate the rich heritage of the budo tradition, it has been my mission to delve deeper through the surface features of martial arts in order to provide students a way to find the "diamonds of life." In my research, I have found that the real beauty of Karate comes from the simplicity and practice of kihon (fundamentals). It is essential that this concept of placing importance on kihon is embraced and practiced as the transformation of one's character becomes apparent; that is, a student may begin their Karate journey with a stagnant character, however with each training session, a polished and vibrant character emerges.

This work has made me reflect on the important aspects of Karate. I was only 32 years old when I wrote this book, and although I have learned much more about Karate since then, I still embrace the basic principles that I feel are important for anyone pursuing the martial arts journey. I have included chapters on the importance of incorporating proper attitudes and habits while training, formalities and etiquettes, and even some worthy suggestions for parents. Other chapters include the basic principles of blocking, striking, thrusting, and kicking techniques. I have stressed the importance of kata, a structured practice of formal patterns or "the way of doing" that enables one to build inner strength and courage and be able to defend themselves from the struggles of daily life. In today's ever-changing world, there is still hope for sanity, goodness, wisdom and spirituality.

Through Karate, it is my hope that these strong foundational components are learned, embraced, and practiced during the storms of adversity, helping to instill and maintain a sense of dignity and honor in one's life.

From the first beginning of my training in Sunset Beach, on the North Shore of Oahu...

...to over 60 years of continuous practice and teaching in a place I now call home in Grants Pass, Oregon, this Karate journey has been a tremendous blessing for me.

CONTENTS

"True Karate is this: that in daily life one's mind and body be trained and developed in a spirit of humility, and that in critical times, one be devoted utterly to the cause of justice." — Gichin Funakoshi

"Karate is a lifetime study." - Kenwa Mabuni

INTRODUCTION TO KARATE-DO

"Karate is like boiling water, if not given continuous heat, it soon becomes cold."
- from Shotos "Twenty Quotes"

Centuries have passed since the original art of Karate was formed. In recent years, especially since the late 1960s, the popularity of Karate has grown and prospered tremendously. In recent decades, many of the concepts and much of the philosophy of this art have been altered or changed. Many of these changes have been beneficial to the Karate practitioner. However, some changes have hindered the progress of the art. There's an old saying that captures the heart of Karate-do: "Karate begins and ends with courtesy." Yet, many instructors and students today fail to recognize the importance of discipline and respect. They fail to understand that self restraint and striving to perfect one's character bring freedom. Instead, only the superficial aspects of Karate are taught and practiced. Hence, the true significance of Karate is lost.

In Karate, as in all martial arts, there appears to be but one reliable path to proficiency - practice. By practicing patiently, diligently, and with the proper state of mind, Karate practitioners learn to eliminate errors and which skills should be clarified, rearranged, and strengthened.

Self-Defense

Karate is a martial art of self-defense. The Japanese characters which form the word Karate mean "empty hand." Literally, this means that the Karate practitioner uses his unarmed body to aid him in a reliable system of self-defense.

As a method of self-defense, Karate is probably as old as the human race. However, only in recent years has this method of "empty-hand" defense been viewed from a more scientific approach in which body movement, timing, balance, and even psychology are studied and applied in formulating techniques that are effective against any would-be assailant.

Physical Discipline

Many people have fallen victim to an undisciplined, overindulgent, and stressful society. A look around clearly shows man's poor condition. Disregarding the need to balance our activities with proper exercise creates obesity, chronic back pain, weak and flabby muscles, poor posture, minimal flexibility, lack of endurance, tension, depression and emotional instability.

The superb coordination and stamina required in executing each Karate movement demands the utmost from your body. With training, you will learn to strengthen your body with proper exercises. In time, each part of your body will present a new dimension of conditioning and growth. Learning these skills will aid you in eliminating and preventing a variety of illnesses and other conditions that cause your body to deteriorate. Karate training brings about a great physical high which will overcome any temptation to indulge in drugs, alcohol, or junk food.

Mental Discipline

Self-defense does not in itself create a worthy art. Karate-do involves mental training as well as physical training. It is hoped that the practitioner will open new doors of learning and understanding: that their existence will take greater meaning. After many hours of practice, the meaning of "Kara" (or empty) will change from the literal definition to a deeper, more esthetic meaning - ridding the mind of negative thoughts and feelings thereby creating space for useful actions more worthy of cultivation.

Spiritual Discipline

As harmonious interaction of mind and body evolves, the practitioner will come to realize that we are mere links in the chain of life. Practicing Karate only to prepare for an attack that may never come proves useless. Striving to strengthen one's mind and body only to achieve worldly happiness would also prove useless if death comes tomorrow. One must learn to expand his thoughts beyond the physical realm into the spiritual sphere. Learn to forget yourself and to adapt to the pace of nature, and you will learn to accept the absolute truth. You must study this well.

In America, we have become procrastinators in our search for spiritual commitment. Our spiritual needs, our morality and our beliefs have slipped into an abyss. As it is in religion, so it is in Karate. It is important to act and to involve yourself with the proper attitudes and to find out more about the absolute truth. This is the true basis of Karate-do.

Summary

Only by combining the four areas of Karate - self-defense, physical, mental and spiritual discipline - do we find ourselves true practitioners of Karate-do. And only when applying our full concentration to each of the four disciplines do we find ourselves reaching our goals and becoming whole. Only then do we begin to understand.

"The more understanding you have about Karate, the less you need to change or modify it." - Tsuguo Sakumoto

A BRIEF HISTORY OF KARATE

A precise written history of Karate's evolution does not exist. This is because of the secrecy of its practice, the inability of many masters to transfer their knowledge to an educational system, and the uncertainty of its transformation in its early form. Nevertheless, India's influence on the Oriental combative techniques can be traced.

According to a popular legend, Bodhidharma (Daruma Taishi in Japanese) was born in the Kshatriya or "warrior" cast of India in the sixth century B.C. His father was King Sugandha of southern India who was also a priest. Bodhidharma was raised to assume his father's position, however, being dissatisfied with that role, he set out to China seeking enlightenment. After years of travel and contemplation, his philosophy evolved into Chinese Chan, or what was later recognized by the Japanese as Zen.

Bodhidharma settled at the Shaolin-szu (in Japanese called the Shorinji), a temple in the Honan Province of China. At the Shorinji, Bodhidharma developed a system of combative techniques based on many of the ingredients of India's yoga and kshatriya training. This training is said to have included a form of weaponless fighting called "vajramushti" (or one whose fist is impenetrable).

Shorinji Kempo eventually emerged as the name given for these techniques. History is uncertain whether Bodhidharma actually introduced or began kempo or if kempo already existed in China. Nonetheless, it is clear his influence was significant.

Okinawa-te

A cultural exchange began between the people ol the Fukien Province in southern China and those of the Ryukyu Islands, an archipelago in the Pacific between Kyushu, Japan and Taiwan. During this exchange, it was basically Shorinji Kempo that eventually reached the Ryukyuans. Although Chinese kempo differed slightly from the Okinawan combative techniques, the similarities, as well as the contrasting forms, helped solidify and nurture a form of self defense called "Okinawa te" (or Okinawa hands.)

For centuries Okinawa was at the mercy of her neighbors. She had long been a fiefdom of China and suffered the military and economic ventures of the Japanese. And, it was during the years of arms prohibition that Okinawa-te especially found its strength.

Okinawan overlord Oho Shin, attempting to consolidate his power, ordered the first weapon ban in 1477. Then in 1609, Shimazo, the powerful Daimyo of the Satsuma clan of Kyushu (Japan's southern most island), conquered the Ryukyus and prohibited owning or carrying any type of weapon. Veiling themselves with the innocent name of "te" the Okinawans polished their art in utmost secrecy. These years of arms prohibition produced a tremendous rise in the martial art development.

Although weapons were outlawed, the Okinawans cleverly incorporated common farm implements into their art. Included among the more popular weapons were: the bo, a 6-foot wooden staff; the sai, a forked metal device; nunchaku, wooden flails; the tonfa, a stick with a handle; kama, or sickle; and the eku, or oar.

Finally, in the early 1900s, authorities lifted the martial arts ban, and the Okinawans could at last practice their art without fear of punishment. They even incorporated Karate into the curriculum of the schools, making it possible for everyone to practice the art, not just members of the upper class. As good, peace-loving people, the Okinawans understood their external ability was in direct proportion to their internal balance. Hence, they strove to hone from within the sharpness of their martial art skills.

Gichin Funakoshi (1868 - 1957)

Gichin Funakoshi is recognized as the man most responsible for systematizing modern-day Karate. Funakoshi was born prematurely in Shuri, Okinawa. By his own admission he was "rather a sickly baby" who was not expected to live long. Because of his frail condition, he was "coddled and pampered" by his grandparents. However at age 11, it was Funakoshi's good fortune to meet and begin Karate training under Yasutsune Azato. Master Azato was one of Okinawa's foremost Karate experts. After several years ol training, Funakoshi's health reversed. No longer frail and weak, but strong and robust, he lived to be nearly 90, and never once, he states, was sick or in need of a doctor.

Funakoshi also trained under Itosu "Ankoh" Yasutsune who was considered the equal of Azato in Karate skill. After becoming an expert in his own right, Funakoshi began taking an active role in introducing Karate to the Okinawan public.

In 1917, Master Funakoshi demonstrated Karate at the Butokuden in Kyoto, Japan, the official martial arts center at that time. In 1921 the emperor of Japan visited Okinawa and Master Funakoshi was again selected to demonstrate Karate in the famous Shuri Castle. Again in 1922 he was invited by the Japan Ministry of Education to introduce Karate to the Japanese people at a physical education exposition. Showing a great deal of interest in the art, the Japanese public encouraged Funakoshi to travel throughout Japan to personally teach them the art of Karate. The major university in Japan invited him to set up a Karate curriculum, and hundreds of students began to study under his guidance.

Kenwa Mabuni (1887 - 1954)

During the following years, a number of other Okinawan Karate masters journeyed to Japan to teach their art. One of the more famous masters was Kenwa Mabuni. Like Funakoshi, Mabuni was a member of an old samurai family, and he, too, studied with Itosu (Shishu, 1830 - 1915), master of the Shorinryu school. Here he learned the Pinan, Passai (Bassai Dai), Chinto, Wanshu, Gojyushiho, and Kushanku (Kosokun Dai) katas. In addition, he learned the Jutte, Jion, and Rohai katas, as well. Later, during the early 1920s, Mabuni studied with the master of the Shorei school, Kanryo Higaonna (1845 - 1915), Under Higaonna, he learned the Shisochin, Sanchin, Kururunfa, Tensho, Saifa, Sanseiryu, Seipai, Naha Seisan, and Seienchin forms. From Aragaki, a leading weapons expert, he learned to use the bo, sai, tonfas, nunchaku, nichokama, kusari-kama, nunte, and tempe.

Shito-ryu

Blending the methods of the two schools, Mabuni developed what he first called the "hanko," (or half-hard) style. Later, he changed the name to "Shito," deriving the name from the alternate reading of the ideograms found in the names of his former teachers - "Shi" for the "Ito" of Itosu and "To" for the "Higa" of Higaonna. Shito-ryu was established between 1930, when Mabuni moved permanently from Okinawa to Osaka, Japan, and 1935, when all schools had to declare a name for the styles they practiced under the order of the Butokuden.

Shito-ryu, then, is a blend of the two major fountainheads of modern Karate: Naha-te, represented by Higaonna's shorei or goju styles, and Shuri-te, represented by Itosu's shorin-ryu. It is the oldest official blend in a recognized style of Karate, though many instructors of the past studied at the various major schools. Today, several styles exist that were developed from the two main sources of Karate, but Mabuni's Shito-ryu was the first which was officially recognized as a major style.

Karate-do

In 1931, the Japanese shortened the term "Karate-jutsu" (China-hand technique) to "Karate-do" (empty-hand way). The character "Kara" (meaning China) was replaced by the ideogram meaning "empty." Although "empty" basically means without weapons, Master Funakoshi described empty in these words, "As a mirrored, polished surface reflects whatever stands before it, and as a great valley carries even small sounds, so must the student of Karate render his mind empty of selfishness and wickedness in an effort to react appropriately toward anything he might encounter." Thus, "empty" means to rid the mind of negative thoughts and feelings and to create space for useful actions more worthy of cultivation. Added to this character were the original ideograms for "te" meaning "hands" and "do," meaning "the way." It was at this time that Karate became more worthy of being accepted as an art form rather than one of brutal tendencies.

Tsutomu Ohshima

The first recognized Karate instructor to come to the United States was Tsutomu Ohshima, a pupil of Funakoshi. Ohshima arrived in Los Angeles in 1956, at the age of 26, and began teaching Karate at the Konko Temple.

Since then, hundreds of Karate schools have sprung up in the United States. Some of these schools emphasize the different Japanese styles of Karate, while others emphasize Okinawan, Chinese, Korean, Indonesian, and Polynesian martial art forms.

Today, Karate has spread throughout the world and still grows in popularity. Its purpose should always be to promote a better existence for mankind both spiritually and morally while providing a means of self-defense, competition, sport, and physical exercise.

Kenzo Mabuni

Kenzo Mabuni was the son of the founder of Shito-ryu Karate-do, Kenwa Mabuni.

Born on May 30th, 1927 at Akahira-Machi, Shuri City in Okinawa, his family moved to Osaka City, Japan in 1929 when he was 2 years old and he remained in his father's house. Kenzo Mabuni began his Karate training at the age of 13 and had continued his training for 60 years. He obtained his Shodan (1st Degree Black Belt) on August 1, 1943 from his father and earned the rank of Judan (10th degree Black belt) as well as a respected master throughout the world.

His organization, Nihon Karatedo Kai was founded by his father in 1939. After his father's death in 1952, his mother, Kame Mabuni, came to Kenzo Mabuni and requested that he take over the style. He inherited the responsibility and became the 2nd Governor of Shito Ryu and successor to this organization. His father left him the Shito Ryu name, his complete syllabus, and the dojo with he Association name Nippon Karate Do Kai. All these remain intact until today. He followed his father's syllabus exactly the way it was written down in 1929 and that is why he called his style, "Seito Shito Ryu" or pure, true Shito Ryu.

Kenzo Mabuni passed away on June 26, 2005 in Osaka, Japan. Kenzo Mabuni's eldest daughter, Tsukasa Mabuni now presides over the Seito Shito-ryu Karate-do Kai organization.

Okinawa, birthplace of Karate-do.

A NOTE FOR PARENTS

"Nothing is so strong as gentleness, nothing so gentle as real strength."
\- Francis de Sales

A young tree with many branches but weak roots will not withstand the tests of nature. It is the same with children. To grow strong and endure, they, too, must have solid foundations Through discipline, governed by love and consistency, parents must be careful to provide their children with the balance necessary for healthy growth.

By enrolling your child in the practice of Karate-do, you are strengthening his foundation. From his practice and study, he will learn many important values that relate directly to life and will enable him to face life's many challenges.

In the practice of Karate-do, your child will learn many aspects of dealing with conflict. Psychologically, he will be taught to be aware of strategies, environment and body language, to control his emotions, and he will gain the proper spirit to accomplish his objectives

Physically, he will be able to block, punch, strike, kick, throw, and move with balance, strength, and stamina. To bring favorable equilibrium to his training, your child will constantly be placed in situations that allow him to practice and develop these skills.

In sparring, only certain strikes may be used to specific target areas. He must learn to fight honorably, using polished techniques, rather than brute force. And he will learn to fight with good spirit - not with emotional frustration or anger.

In kata practice, he will battle himself. He will learn to deal with his weaknesses and to have the discipline, patience, and courage required to complete the kata. He will find that much practice is necessary to understand and accept the structure of kata training in order to present a sound interpretation and performance. In kata, as in life, the boundaries are tight yet limitless; his instructor will guide him to worthy and balanced choices.

As the child develops his techniques and becomes confident, his mind will have more room to grow. Encouraged by his promotions, he will not be discouraged by defeat. If he finds that, perhaps, he is not the best, he will know that he can survive amongst the best.

Just as he learns to physically block kicks and punches, so too he will learn to mentally block harsh words and gestures; he will calmly continue the path toward his objectives without letting life disturb or upset him.

Kata training will further his understanding that he is responsible for himself, that he alone must succeed or fail, for there is no one else to blame if things go wrong. Sparring "kumite" will heighten his sense of responsibility for others. He will understand that he must act decisively, but always with control.

When your child needs to speak up for his rights, he will have the confidence to do so, and to do so with wisdom. If he must remain quiet and unobtrusive, he will learn to do this also. As he spends time in the dojo, he will become increasingly sensitive to the needs of others and will find time to give encouragement and compassion, and to share brotherly love.

A wheel turns smoothly on a well-balanced axle, yet if too tightly placed, it becomes choked and function is lost. Parents, in their desire to do things which they feel are good for the child, often place too many restrictions on children and that can be as unbalanced for a child as giving him or her too much freedom. Your task in finding the balance will be endless. Your child's instructor is also obligated to discover that balance. Together, with the support of the sensei, you will have the tools to teach him how to deal with life more fully.

Communication is important with your child's instructor. Make time to meet with the instructor at least once a month to discuss your child's development at home, in school, and at the dojo.

Periodically, most children feel compelled to test their limits. If your child enters one of these periods, choose not to use his Karate training as leverage. You would not discipline your child by removing him from school, nor should you restrict him from other healthy activities that promote good habits. Other disciplinary actions should be found. At the dojo, your child's instructor may not let him test for promotion during the remainder of the quarter, or may restrict his tournament participation. But his regular training for daily growth is vital and should not be affected.

Should your child appear to be losing interest in Karate training, try to determine what is really taking place. Perhaps another student (usually in beginners' classes) is placing unnecessary pressure on your child. This can easily be resolved if you bring it to the instructor's attention. You may feel your son or daughter wants to stop training because of other demands that may be equally positive for growth. Then perhaps you may want to stop your child's training for a time to allow exploration in these other fields of interest.

However, more often than not, a student's desire to stop training is motivated by laziness and lack of self-discipline. Naturally, you will not hear the real reason. But, you will hear numerous excuses designed to win your approval. If you feel this is the real reason for his lack of interest, simply tell him that choosing to quit is not an option. Often, you'll see amazing results even if there is a bit of rebellion in the beginning.

Lastly, but still vitally important, I must encourage you to take an active part in your child's training. Encourage him. Ask him to demonstrate what he has learned. Attend his class. You may not want to watch your child in every class (and you may have to bite your tongue when you do watch), but occasionally, you should plan on staying for the entire session. Other events such as tournaments and class outings can become occasions and opportunities for entire family outings which show added encouragement and a sense of love and caring to your child.

Your child's involvement in Karate-do will help you nourish him. His decisions will be sound, his mind composed. He'll see life through eyes more focused; his hearing will attune to gentle sounds like the soft breeze passing amidst a beautiful pine that has many fine branches and a strong foundation.

Proper Karate practice enables students to face life's many challenges.

Daily routines help children feel safe and secure, while developing a lifelong love of learning.

PHILOSOPHY

One of the most important aspects of Karate is the philosophy behind the physical movements. Just as one must have physical balance, one must have a well-balanced philosophical attitude. If this is lacking, the products of our thoughts become weak and have no value. With correct practice, the space that is often filled with emotional blocks such as anger, fear, and frustration will be replaced with spirit, confidence, and motivation. We are then able to create worthy and useful life skills.

Lao Tzu, a Taoist sage, explained this idea beautifully. He wrote:
*"Thirty spokes share the wheel's hub; it is the center
which makes it useful. Shape clay into a vessel; it is
the space within which makes it useful. Cut doors
and windows for a room; it is the holes which make
them useful. Therefore, profit comes from what is
there, usefulness from what is not."*

Meditation is one of the bases for creating mental framework for the space within. This practice teaches you to fill your mind with a positive attitude. This makes it possible to act without recourse to reasoning or allowing interference. You will be one with nature rather than vainly trying to conquer it.

By keeping a wholesome philosophy and practicing meditation daily, you begin to increase your inner strength and reap many blessings.

Spiritual Aspects

Many students inquire, "How does Karate fit in with the doctrine of Christianity and Western culture, being from an Eastern culture and Oriental background?"

Eastern culture is strongly influenced by Buddhism and Shintoism. These religions are good, positive religions which promotes humanity's higher qualities. They do not differ from Christianity in that respect.

Japan has long been influenced by Shintoism and Bushido or "The Way of the Warrior." The basic tenets of both Shintoism and Bushido call for a loyalty to one's country, family, and friends, as well as an understanding and control of one's self and a deep appreciation of nature. Again, these percepts do not discernibly differ from the beliefs found in Western culture.

Karate is an art which can promote inner growth. By applying the discipline developed in the study of Karate-do, one creates a unity of mind, body, and spirit. The practice of Karate leads one to an understanding of unity in a physical sense, and also allows them to seek higher spiritual understanding. This art can be applied regardless of religious faith or back ground.

Karate does not promote any religion. However, being a Christian, much of my teaching and philosophy connects directly to the Word of God as given to us in the Bible. It is not the purpose of Karate-do to take the place of religion but to augment religion in one's search for wholeness and truth.

Just as there are many religions, there are many schools of Karate. Some styles and schools are good, and some are cultish and lack quality and depth. One must choose the best for them, determining which fits his needs, then apply these elements to his whole life, as he would apply the elements of religion in his everyday existence.

Young people grow strong mentally and physically while learning the importance of working in harmony with others.

"The power of youth is the common wealth for the entire world..."

TRAINING WITH PROPER ATTITUDES AND HABITS

"Half of our mistakes in life arise from feeling when we ought to think, and thinking when we ought to feel."
- Churton Collins

Realistic Expectations

Too many students practice Karate expecting some kind of miraculous transformation with only a few months training. They think they will be able to destroy any adversary with a single blow, and that people will be awed by, and thereby attribute greatness to them. This is, of course, nonsense. Attitudes of this type are promoted by fantastic stories and outrageous, irresponsible movies that have invaded theaters and homes nationwide.

Karate training extends over one's lifetime. One cannot learn - let alone master - all there is to know within a few months. Good and worthy qualities come through time and effort. They must be cultivated. Karate is no different. A true Karate-ka will make a complex kata "look" simple; his kumite will "look" strong, yet effortless. Don't be deceived - such excellence is achieved - only through serious practice.

From the beginning, it is most important you form worthwhile training habits which will help you develop and grow steadily. It is unfortunate that, too often, students overexert themselves only to find they are weary and stagnant. They quit, having learned but the superficial aspects of Karate training. One must train systematically with realistic expectations. Even if one is taught only a few katas at a time, he should practice wholeheartedly, searching for a depth of purpose in each kata.

Priorities

Misplaced priorities commonly cause a student to lapse into weariness and fall behind. Priorities such as work, school, or family endeavors are important considerations, and scheduling conflicts can cause a student to miss training sessions. However, most of these conflicts can be worked out with the instructor. More often than not, these outside "priorities" are leisure pursuits such as social time, parties, movies, a call to laziness, too much computer gaming, and other non-pressing opportunities.

The student misses a few training sessions, begins lagging behind, and is unable to keep up with the performance of his group. He may also become weary because he only does his Karate practice at the dojo, saying he doesn't have time to practice at home. Thus, he lacks endurance. And, because he has been gone, he never retains enough to carry him through the next class session, then becomes so conscious of his inability to perform adequately that he finds his training is no longer enjoyable.

Occasionally a student becomes ill and unable to attend class. This is a legitimate reason for missing training. However, the point remains, if he misses class, he falls behind. During illness, one helpful practice is for him to review his notebook. This would be helpful in remembering techniques and class discussions that may have faded from memory. Calling a fellow student to find out what has been taking place in class is also helpful. This will, at least, help him keep mentally in tune with Karate training.

Training with Spirit

Many people are up one day and down the next. Their spirit - and their lives - are out of balance. A deep river has a strong, steady current. It does not rush madly one moment harming things in its path only to round a bend and become low and stagnant. Its flow is even. Strive to keep your spirit steady and centered, neither too high nor too low.

In the dojo, study your spirit. Do you train hard one day and poorly the next? You should not have to "call" on your spirit when you spar or perform your kata, it should be evident in everything you do. Resolve to do each movement of exercise to the best of your ability, from meditation to sit-ups and push ups, and each technique in each kata. Bring to bear as much self-discipline as possible in the dojo. You will learn and grow; your body and mind will become strong.

Extend yourself and your spirit. To train hard only for promotions, trophies, and tournament victories is shallow. You must set goals and work steadily each day to meet them. Students must learn to communicate with their sensei and try constantly to understand and savor the core of Karate-do.

To think only of yourself is equally shallow. An advanced student's kata may improve; his kumite may become stronger. But if he takes no time to help new students grow, if he extends only his ego in sparring drills, then he is learning nothing about Karate-do. His growth is stunted.

Little things count. Take time to learn the names of your fellow students. Get to know them. If necessary, older and advanced students should help monitor the dojo. For instance, sometimes the young ones need a kind reminder that the dojo is a place of respect, not a playground. Also, advanced students should lead cleanup efforts at the end of each class. Remember, when you extend your proper spirit, you enrich those around you. This increases your value and that of the class.

Summary

Diet, and practicing good habits in all a student does, play an important role in the outcome of Karate training. If an unhealthy diet is consumed, or if one drinks or smokes excessively, uses mind-altering drugs, or gets insufficient sleep, he will find it most difficult to keep up with training.

Students should initiate proper attitudes and habits conducive to the principles of Karate-do. Place your priorities accordingly, and do not give in to temptations that are only enjoyable for the moment. When one's time is budgeted wisely, there will be plenty of time to enjoy life without hampering Karate training.

Kata practice aligns students with good habits and strong spirit.

Each technique is thoroughly explained and demonstrated to make learning easier.

Resolve to do each movement to the best of your ability.

DOJO FORMALITIES AND ETIQUETTE

Tradition forms the nucleus and backbone of Karate-do. To maintain and preserve this tradition, it is important that students become aware of dojo formalities and etiquette.

Whenever entering or leaving the dojo, students should pause momentarily at the entrance and bow facing the interior of the dojo. The bow demonstrates respect for the place where people from all walks of life gather together to train and grow while creating stronger values for themselves.

Whenever black belts are in the dojo and class has not yet begun, students should greet them with a bow.

At the beginning of each class, students will line up according to rank, generally with the highest ranking member to the right. At times, the instructors may wish the highest ranking member to line up to the left for practical reasons due to the dojo's structural design.

Once students have lined up in rank, meditation will follow. This is done in the "seiza" position. At the command "Mokuso," all students will pause briefly to rid their minds of negative thoughts and to achieve a state of readiness for the ensuing lesson.

At the command, "Shomen ni, rei," given by the highest ranking student on the extreme right, students will place their hands on the floor and bow until their foreheads are just above the floor. After pausing momentarily to show respect to the place of training, students will resume the kneeling, or seiza, position. The senior student will then give the command, "Sensei ni, rei," at which time students will bow facing their instructor. Again, they resume the kneeling position and remain calm and attentive until the next command of "Otagai ni rei' is given, at which time students will pair off and bow to each other.

At the end of each training session, students will again line up for meditation. After meditating, the senior student will give the command, "Otagai ni, rei." The next command is " Sensei ni rei, followed by "Shomen ni, rei." After this bow is completed, students will remain in the kneeling position facing the front of the dojo for the sensei to complete his closing comments,

Prior to leaving the dojo, it is respectful for students to bow to all senior black belts.

Other Formalities and Rules of Etiquette:
1. Whenever the instructor calls upon a student to demonstrate a technique, he will bow before and after the demonstration.
2. When a student pairs up with another student, bow to each other before and after the practice.
3. Students should bow and greet their sensei at all dojo activities and tournaments.
4. When coming to class late, students should meditate and exercise briefly before joining the class, making as little disturbance as possible.
5. If children or friends are invited to observe class, they should be briefed regarding the need for respectful behavior before they arrive at the dojo.
6. After each class, all students should participate in clean-up activities, such as wiping down the mats.
7. Gis should be fresh and clean at all times.
8. Instructors should be addressed as sensei at all times in the dojo.

The bow demonstrates respect for others, as well as respect for yourself.

Folding the Gi

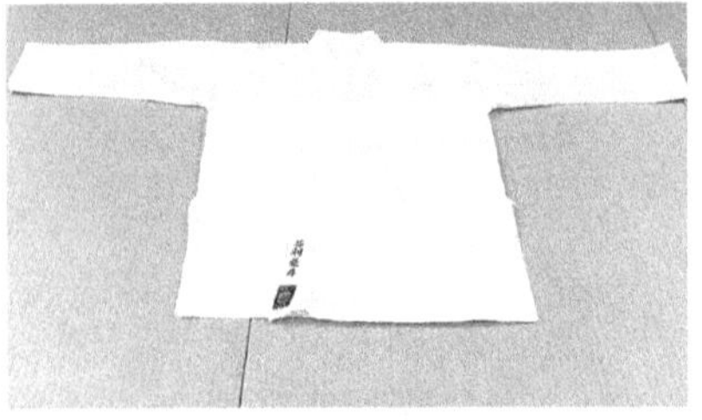 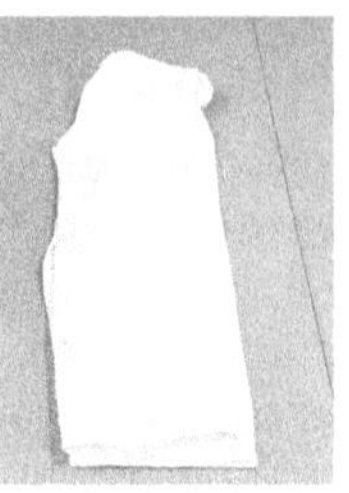 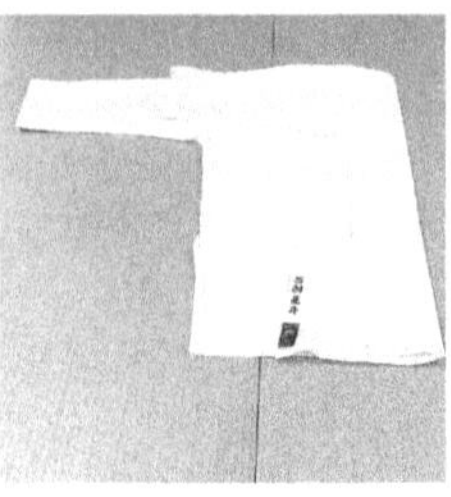

Fold jacket in half. The fold in sleeves pressing firmly each time to eliminate wrinkles.

Fold gi pants.

Place pants under one end of jacket.

 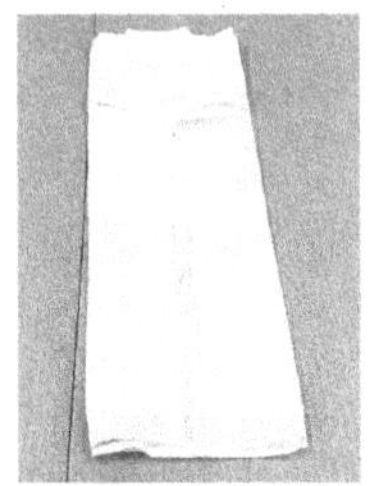  

Fold sleeves and jacket, pressing firmly each time to eliminate wrinkles.

Fold gi in thirds.

Secure belt around folded gi and carry over your shoulder.

Be sure to unfold your gi after each workout and hang to air dry and to keep it from wrinkling. Always keep your gi clean and wash it frequently.

It is recommended to have two training gis.

Wearing a gi has many wholesome benefits:
It promotes commonality among the students and gives them a sense of belonging.
It gives students a sense of community and respect.
It helps students stay focused, motivated, and confident.
It symbolizes and represents the identity of a martial artist.
It stands for their organization's principles and identity.

MEDITATION

Meditation is one of the more difficult, and, perhaps, misunderstood phases of Karate-do training. At the same time, however, it is one of Karate training's most essential and beneficial elements.

Man lives in a highly sophisticated, technological environment of his own creation. Our minds are constantly besieged as one voice after another demands our attention. The assault comes from cell phones, the internet, social media, television, radio, newspapers, and magazines. It comes from teachers, parents, and friends. As more knowledge is acquired, greater is the amount of "information" thrown at us - and the faster we scramble to keep pace. As the pace of life grows increasingly hectic, our attention spans grow shorter. Respite is rare. For many, even sleep is difficult and disturbed. Our society is trapped in this insane circle.

As we continue to distance ourselves from nature's rhythm, the more we resemble lemmings in a mad rush to the cliffs, our minds filled with negativity, and self-destructive thoughts we cannot control.

Purpose

Meditation helps open the doors to a more peaceful coexistence with the universe. It quiets the mind. It creates not a blank or empty mind, but a calm, silent mind, not a "state" of mind, but a tranquil "beginner's" mind.

Position

One way to practice meditation is to assume the "seiza" position. In seiza, you sit on your knees, your weight resting on the lower legs and heels. Your hands rest palm down on your thighs, as you sit with your back straight. Your surroundings are quiet and clean, your conscience is clear. You may choose to close your eyes at first, but in the more advanced stages of meditation you will slightly open your eyes. You will learn to gaze at a spot a few feet in front of you without really focusing on that spot. Instead, you will focus on your breathing.

Breathing

When meditating, focus on your breathing and your mind will follow. Your idle thoughts, worries, and the pressures of the day will not persist. Inhale slowly and quietly through the nose. Do this deeply, so you feel your diaphram expand and fill with air. Exhale slowly and quietly through the mouth. Do this completely, until the last bit of air is gone and the dia-phram is empty. Relax, but focus tightly on your breathing as you continue to deeply inhale and exhale.

Benefits

Through meditation you will stabilize your mind. You see in the world around you what the mind creates when it lacks stability. When all the debris of your conscious mind is set aside, you will begin to "see" things as they really are and act more wisely. Each of us has a purpose to fulfill and this can only be accomplished in a positive way only through proper focus. Meditation will allow you to flow with nature and help your mind expand. As this occurs, you become a more positive, nurturing force.

Summary

Be practical about meditation. You are not trying to separate mind from body. You are trying to unite them in a wholesome manner. "You should not lose your self-sufficient mind," said Suzuki, a Zen master. In Japanese there is the term "shoshin," or "beginner's mind." This does not mean an ignorant or closed mind, but one that is fresh and ready, one that sees many possibilities. Meditation must be practiced sincerely.

Meditation helps create a calm, quiet mind.

WARM UP EXERCISES

In the Beginning

If a beginning runner tried to run a four-minute mile in his first race, the effort would be foolish, the results predictable. He would suffer greatly and probably complete less than a quarter of the race before falling into exhaustion, or worse. And the physical pain of such a ridiculous effort would linger.

Even if a runner was fast, experienced, and in great condition- even in "world class" condition - he would not think of running without first warming up and stretching thoroughly. You must understand it is the same in martial arts, regardless of rank or ability.

It is a well-known fact that Karate training will build excellent overall physical conditioning. The key word here is "build." This occurs over time, not in a few days. In a few months you become stronger, but this process should be even and gradual.

In the beginning, it is especially important to know your limitations. You must listen to your body, but you must not lie to yourself. Stay within your personal boundaries. But remember, to grow strong you must strive to extend those boundaries. It is a fine line.

Avoiding Injury

Muscles and ligaments must be thoroughly warm before they are used in strenuous activity. To avoid injury, students must practice their exercises seriously. If you do so, within a few months you'll notice your muscle resistance has become less intense and painful. You'll also discover that your ability to stretch and bend has increased beyond belief.

Among the calisthenics popular today are some exercises that stretch the body in an unnatural way. Your instructor will point these out, and they are to be avoided, especially when practicing at home. The objective is to increase and maintain suppleness, to stimulate a better flow of blood and oxygen, and to create a healthy mental and physical state.

Warming up may also be done with a partner. This is encouraged. With a partner, you are not only able to stretch each other, but you're also able to observe one another to assure the exercises are performed properly.

During exercise, try to relax physically and mentally. Perform each exercise in gradual stages, and keep breathing naturally. Avoid hazardous exercises, and remember that loosening the muscles will bring added agility which enables you to perform Karate techniques with much greater ease, fluidity, and understanding.

The Exercises
1. Jumping jacks or running in place gets the blood circulating through the muscles. This is very important to avoid strain.
2. Neck circles.
3. Standing trunk stretching, first side to side, then forward and backward, then in a circular motion.
4. Sitting trunk stretching.
5. Knee and ankle loosening.
6. Finger, wrist and arm loosening.
7. Sitting leg stretching.
8. Push-ups.
9. Situps.
10. Leg lifts, forward, to the side, and back.

Other Considerations
I. If you're in the dojo prior to the beginning of class, warm up carefully on your own before practicing your kata or techniques.
2. At times, more advanced students will be asked to warm-up on their own. At such times, do not avoid exercising because you think no one is watching. Warming exercises are not punishment. They protect you and help your body grow supple and strong.
3. Your sensei may ask you to lead warm ups. If so, realize being young or old, male or female makes no difference. It's simply a responsibility you must take seriously.
4. In cold or damp weather, your muscles and ligaments are tighter. During such times, it is wise to spend more time warming up and loosening.
5. Conditioning plays a major role in any sport. Many football games are won in the fourth quarter simply because of one team's superior physical condition. Develop a regular exercise program that you can do at least three times a week outside the dojo. Your sensei will gladly offer suggestions and guidance to help you develop a sound, healthy program. Such a program will provide many benefits in your daily life, and you will notice an increased performance in the dojo as well.
6. After learning proper stretching techniques, try to make time each day to stretch. This can be done while watching television. The benefits are immeasurable.

Senior students take the initiative to begin warm ups at the beginning of each class.

Jumping rope

Kettlebell

Ladder drills

Hitting the heavy bag

Push-ups

Rope climbing

FUNDAMENTALS

It is the same with fundamentals. If you fail to master little things - the basics - your performance will bear a scar that grows with time.

Working on the basics is probably the most important aspect of Karate practice. This is where habits are formed. Unless students learn each technique on a scientific basis under supervision from a qualified instructor employing a systematic, properly scheduled training program, the student's efforts will be in vain. Likewise, without the student's serious effort, concentration, and focus, the instructor's efforts will be in vain.

Karate-do is an art. Diligence is necessary to become proficient. This point is critical: Never be afraid to ask questions. Bad habits are like fleas, easy to acquire but most difficult to get rid of.

Form

In fundamentals practice you will be taught the physics and physiology of the moves. The instructor will point out the importance of form. With correct form you will begin to realize the effectiveness of each movement. In golf, correct swing form is a must in order to achieve accuracy, control, and power in hitting the ball. Tennis players spend hours of practice trying to create the good form necessary to hit the ball properly. In Karate practice, form is especially important in that it enables the student to achieve strong, effective techniques that one day may be needed not just for sport, but for self-defense.

Balance and Center of Gravity

In practice you will be given many fundamentals to help you create better balance and a stronger center of gravity. Here, various stances are emphasized. Some enhance your stability, which increases your continuing effectiveness. Others increase your ability to move swiftly in any direction. Students will notice that their center of gravity shifts constantly from being evenly distributed over each foot to the extremes of being over one foot or the other. The position of your legs is important, as they act either to support you for increased balance or to absorb the shock of your opponent's actions.

Power and Speed

Only after correct form and balance are achieved should power and speed be emphasized. Techniques achieve their power by concentration of maximum force at a focused point. The concentration of the force is not effective without speed. You will understand this when striking the bag or makiwara (punching board). Other training, such as lifting weights, is not really necessary unless your instructor counsels you to do so. In Karate, the objective is not to hit or move a powerful object slowly, but rather to strike a small target quickly. Your training must be conducive to this concept.

Hip Coordination

Speed and power will be maximized with proper hip movement. When punching without emphasizing hip coordination, you will feel restricted and a quick loss of energy will result. However, if the power concentrated in the hips is transmitted in the execution of each punch, you will notice the added surge of power that is created by a more thorough, complete body movement.

Focus

Your instructor will constantly remind you of focus. It is important that you understand what this means. Focusing your techniques can be achieved by understanding muscle relaxation and tension. If you are to respond quickly to the constantly changing situations in sparring, you must learn to keep your body relaxed. At the instant of focus, or the point where your power is concentrated, your muscles are tense and then instantly relaxed to prepare for your next action. Practicing this constant tensing and relaxing of the body will enhance the beauty of your Karate performance.

Rhythm

Rhythm is also an important factor in fundamental training. The proper execution of combinations, or a series of movements, will be obtained through proper rhythm training. You must learn the degree of focus needed to be used and carried from one technique to another in order to have a smooth, flowing transition of body movements.

Rhythm is especially essential in kata practice. As in all creative dances, you must practice all of the ingredients to achieve rhythm. Apply strength and focus at the correct time; apply speed in each movement and from movement to movement; make smooth transitions from one movement to the next.

With the understanding of rhythm, you will be able to achieve a higher degree of technical success, creativity and beauty in Karate.

Timing and Distance

Regardless of all other factors, the application of each technique in combat will prove effective only if your timing and distance are precise. All your strength and technique, no matter how powerful, will prove useless if applied at the wrong time.

Distance directly correlates with timing. Your target area will constantly be moving, and it is necessary to accurately judge distance. Your instructor will demonstrate this and help you become proficient when practicing prearranged and free sparring.

Spirit

Practicing Karate fundamentals may prove frustrating at times. Little things go wrong, expectations are not fulfilled, or you may not learn a kata as fast as you'd like. When frustrated, students tend to find fault with something in the dojo - other students or the instructor - and begin creating excuses to quit training.

Karate practice will teach you how to defend yourself against an adversary, but you must use your self-defense skills only in the most extreme circumstances. Realistically, such circumstances should be rare. If you can understand this fundamental point of Karate-do, your ability to withstand such frustration will increase greatly.

In order to achieve your higher goals, spirit must always be prevalent. This should be tempered and supported by compassion, understanding, and consideration of others. With these concepts in mind, you will create an atmosphere for unimagined personal growth.

To sustain your spirit in class, practice with an attitude of acceptance and trust. Keep an open mind, and follow instructions carefully and wholeheartedly. Always give your best.

Summary

Begin your Karate training with good habits in the fundamentals. Concentrate on your form, balance, and center of gravity. Combine speed, power, and focus with rhythm, timing, and hip coordination. Study your spirit. Keep it strong and level; bring it to bear on all you do. If you fully concentrate on these concepts, your body, mind, and spirit will begin to soar.

UKE NO GO GENSOKU

(Shito-Ryu Five Methods of Defense)

Kenwa Mabuni, the founder of Shito-Ryu, defined five principles of blocking:

Rakka: (Blossoms Fall from a Shaking Tree)
Blocking with such tremendous force as to knock the blossoms from its branches.

Ryusui: (Two Rivers Join in Harmony)
The meeting of two rivers that together create a force greater than each alone, and doing so with little or no turbulence.

Teni: (A Willow Sways in the Wind)
The branches of a willow tree that sway to and fro in the wind allowing its tremendous force to pass seemingly effortlessly. The concept is to shift the body (taisabaki) or turning away from an attack to avoid the direct force of the attack,

Kushin: (The Lion Crouches Low in the Grass)
Likened to a lion that crouches unnoticeably in the grass, ready to spring an attack on its prey. The stances may be disguised to shift quickly out of one stance and into another (typically at an angle), and then pounce on the attacker's unguarded moment.

Hangeki: (A Flower Greets the Morning Sun)
A flower opens its petals early in the morning to accept the rays of the sun for nourishment. Greet the opponent's actions with a counter-attack to neutralize the action and to defeat his aggression.

REFLEXES AND KARATE

This section examines some of the reflexes and reactions that occur during Karate practice.

Technically, reflexes are the result of involuntary activity. These involuntary reactions may be altered in some instances. When surprised with a strike, most people will flail wildly with their arms, blink, and try to evade in an erratic manner that is involuntary. Through training, the involuntary may be replaced with the voluntary. In other words, the individual may respond with an appropriate block or a well-timed counter strike.

Transmission of the Reflex Signal

Nerves send messages to the brain and spinal cord, and nerve endings are connected by synapses. The synapse, or point of contact between nerve endings, passes the electricity or stimulus from one nerve to the next. The electrical charge is created by stimulating the nerve, for example with pain. The nerve then fires and passes its charge to either the spinal cord, the brain, or both. These principals are fairly well known, but this mechanism contains two important points.

First, a chemical reaction helps pass the charge from one nerve to the next. It is commonly known that temperature greatly affects how chemicals interact. Warmer temperatures quicken reactions and cold temperatures slow them down. It's been proven that human reflexes are significantly faster during warm conditions. Therefore, wear warm clothing while waiting to spar at tournaments. If you are cold, expect to be slower.

Second, a proper amount of stimulation is necessary before the nerve will fire. Touching a lukewarm stove will not cause your hand to jerk away. Enough heat must be present in order to cause the response. It is a physiological law that if many small stimuli are applied rapidly, they will compound until the nerve fires. This is called summation. For example, let's place heat on a scale of one to ten. And, let's assume that eight is hot enough to make one jerk his hand away from the stove, but six is not enough to cause the same response. However, several sixes in quick succession would create enough stimulus to cause one to jerk his hand away.

This may be applied to kumite which is a high or cortical level of reflex. If you over prepare to counterattack, the nerves to one's arm become loaded with small impulses. Then, when the time is right to counter your opponent, a faster than usual reaction is possible.

Spinal Level Reflexes

These reflexes are virtually automatic and occur instantly. Most of these reflexes are protective in nature.

Golgi Tendon Reflex: Sensory nerves working with the tendons control this reflex. A good example of this is when you step off a curb unexpectedly and your knees buckle. In other words, this reflex unlocks joints in the event of sudden extreme stress by a continuous monitoring of tendon/muscle tension. This sudden relaxation of the entire muscle is the lengthening reaction.

Stretch Reflex: The myotactic reflex is the stretch reflex. This reflex is a response of a muscle to stretch beyond its present length. Thus, if in kumite, if one surprises his opponent by grasping and pulling the opponent's arm, the opponent will jerk his arm back in an instantaneous protective movement allowing an opening for the attacker to score. The element of surprise will be all one needs to take advantage of the opponent's protective reflex.

Rebound Reflex: Another interesting phenomena regarding spinal level reflexes is called the rebound reflex. Reflexes fatigue rapidly. This means that immediately after a reflex ends, a second reflex is much more difficult to elicit. This explains why someone who is faked even slightly out of position is "frozen" for just a split second while the real strike is delivered. Therefore, it is quite effective to use the same strike that was used as a fake.

Muscle Spasm: Muscle spasms, or cramps, result from locally irritating factors such as severe cold, lack of blood flow to the muscle, over exercise of the muscle, or a reaction to a sharp blow. These cause pain, which causes a muscle contraction, which creates more pain and acts to increase the contraction. A small irritation may, in this way, cause a full-blown muscle spasm. Merely counter flexing the muscle may completely cure the pain.

Low Brain Level Reflexes

These are subconscious functions of the body. They deal with such things as arterial blood pressure and respiration.

High Brain or Cortical Level Reflexes

These reflexes are the ultimate reaction to a stimulus. It is where sight, sound, and touch are interpreted for a stimulus to react. This level of reflex is abstract in a sense, because thought elicits a response such as a punch or a kick.

When one begins Karate, each move must be interpreted and purposefully performed. Soon, patterns begin to form on the subconscious level. Reactions are faster than thoughts. This is why reactions must be carefully controlled. For example, one won't punch until ready, but when ready, the punch is controlled on a subconscious level regarding focus, control, power, and speed. Then the process of learning each subconscious reflex in the proper form begins. This process never ends and is a difficult task. All these memorized reactions must be continually altered and then put into proper form, and then learned again on a subconscious level. The ultimate result is to have automatic levels of proper form.

Through kata practice your positive reflexes become more natural.

PSYCHOLOGICAL PRINCIPLES

Psychology plays an important role in Karate. In order to become victorious in any battle, including the internal battle with yourself, you must learn to meet each task without fear or negative thoughts. One must learn to identify what the dangers are and react instinctively and appropriately, and at the same time be guided by a calm, contemplative mind. Especially in kumite, one must learn to achieve a mental attitude that will enable effective reactions. To create or allow an unbalanced mind leads to frustration or even destruction.

Ancient Karate masters handed down the term "mizu no kokoro" which means "a mind like water." What this means is keeping the mind calm and reflective - like an undisturbed body of water. By practicing this concept, you will be able to see the objectives of your opponent. The calmer your mind, the better your chances are of responding to his attacks, whether they be physical or psychological, in a positive manner.

You must, then, strive to have a clear, contemplative mind, one that reflects the true images as they occur. This is necessary if you are to capably and appropriately respond to any situation.

If your mind is calm and focused, your chances of defending yourself increase greatly.

STANCES

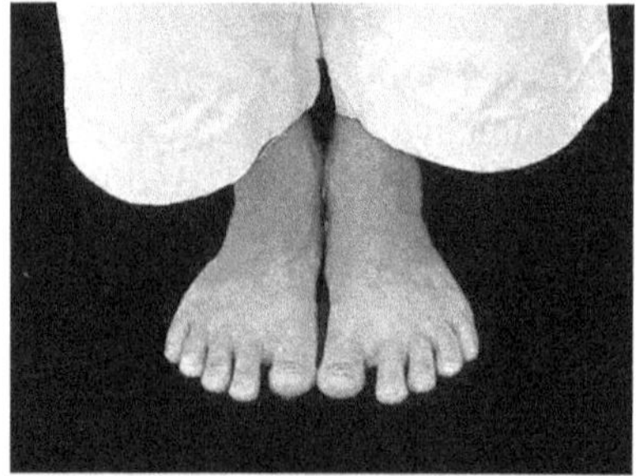

Heisoku dachi

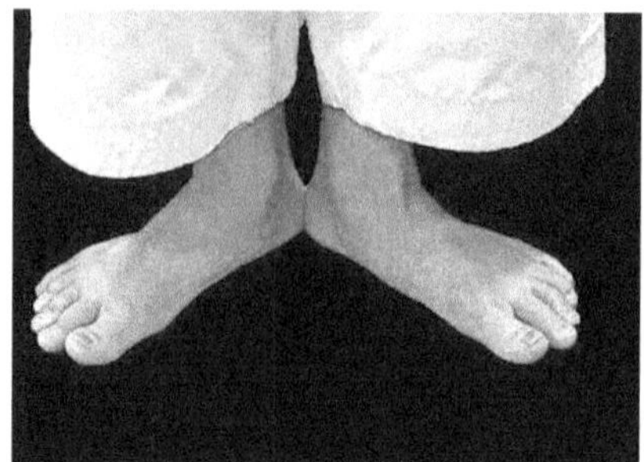

Musubi dachi

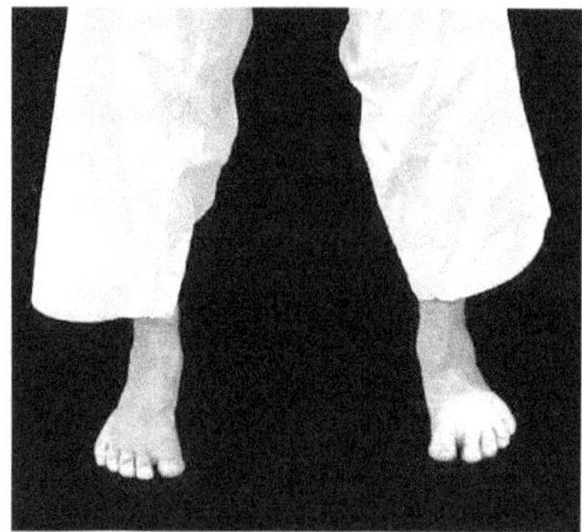

Hachiji dachi

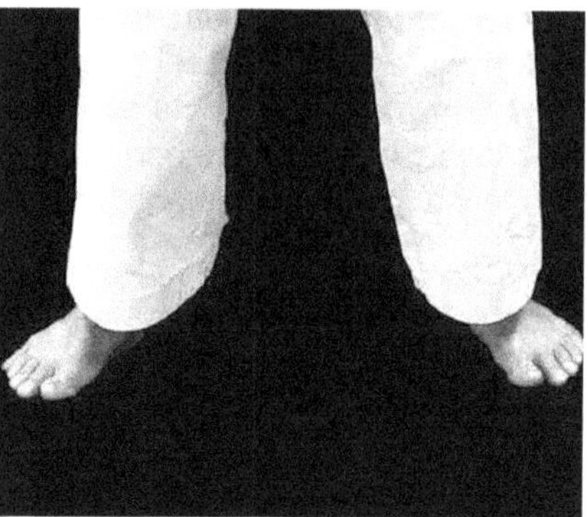

Soto hachiji dachi

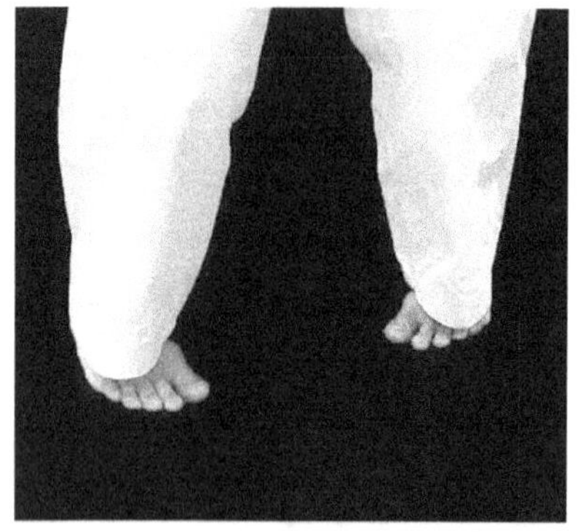

Sanchin dachi

Uchi hachiji dachi

STANCES (continued)

Shiko dachi

Kosa dachi

Kokutsu dachi

Nekoashi dachi

Zenkutsu dachi

Sagiashi dachi

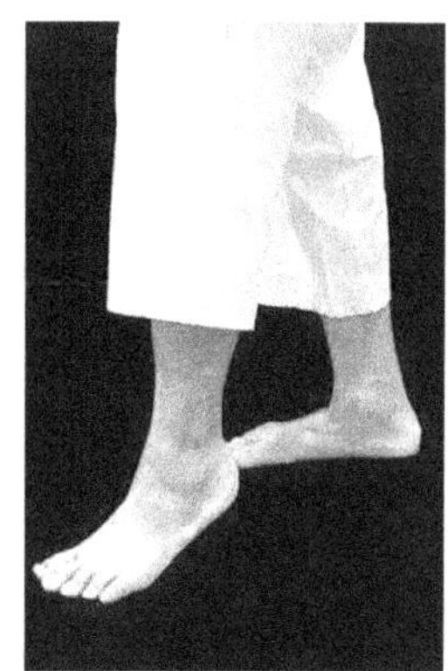

Renoji dachi

BLOCKS

(Some of the names have changed for these blocks)

Jodan age uke

Soto uke

Naka uke

Harai uke

Ude uke

Shuto uke

Kosa uke

Hiji sasae uke

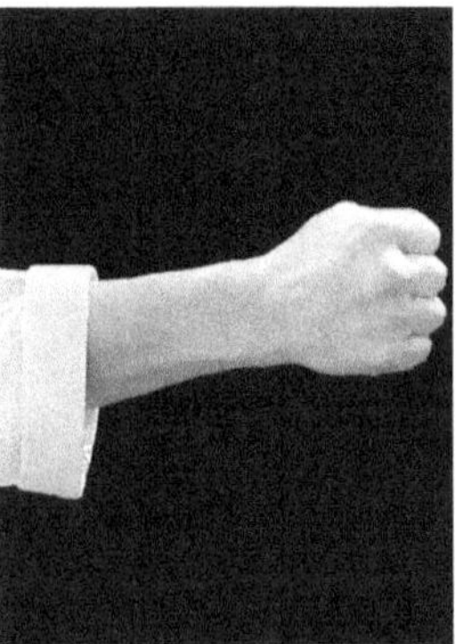

Kentsui uke

BLOCKS (continued)

Ninoude uke

Hirayuki

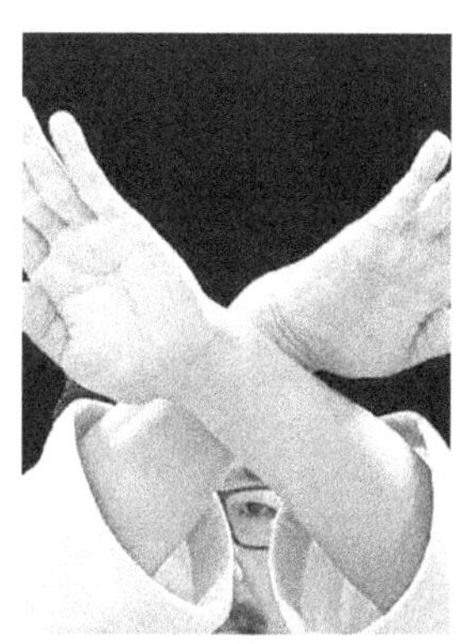

Kosa uke

Kakete uke

Ken sasae uke

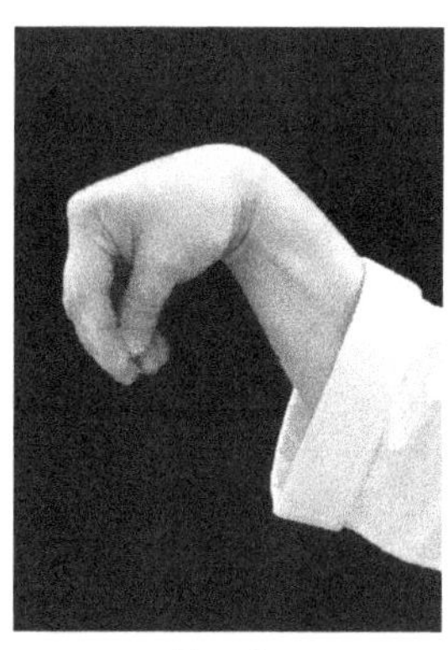

Ko uke

Gassho uke

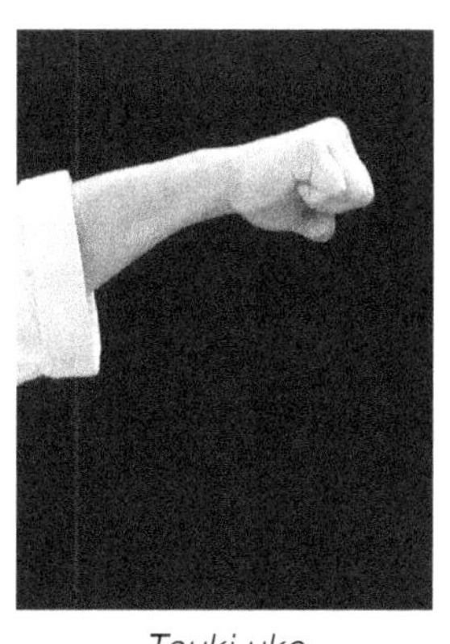

Tsuki uke

Kakiwake uke

BLOCKS (continued)

Oura uke

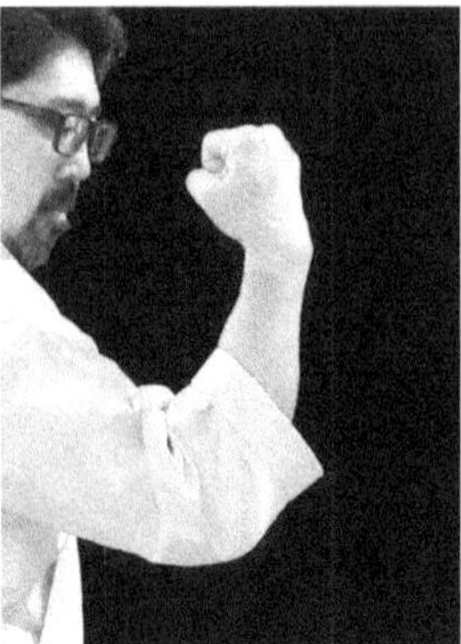

Hiji otoshi uke

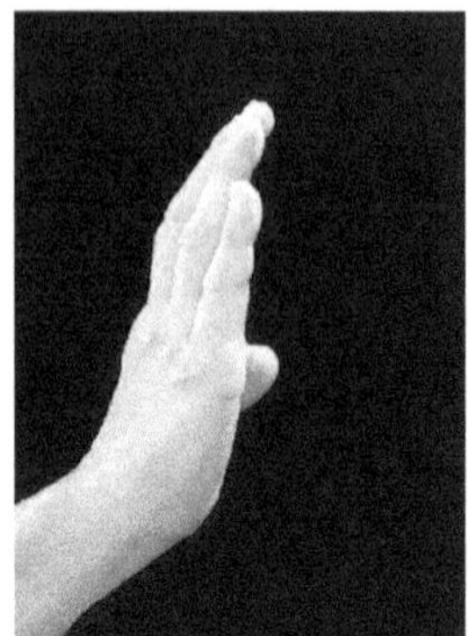

Seryuto uke

Sukui uke

Sukuidome uke

Teisho uke

Wa uke

Many parts of the body become useful tools for self-defense.

Karate training improves dynamic balance performance reducing potential injuries.

STRIKES

Shuto uchi, palm down

Hira basami

Nukite

Ken uchi

Hiji ate

Teisho uchi

Oyayubi uchi

Ko uchi

Shuto uchi, palm up

STRIKES (continued)

Uraken uchi

Ryōte mimi hyōshi uchi

Haito uchi

Washide uchi

The goal of these strikes is to develop a coordinated, powerful technique using the proper stances, hips, and entire body movement to hit vulnerable targets. This allows a smaller person to strike using their body weight toward a larger potential attacker.

KICKS

Yoko geri

Mae Kekomi geri

Kakato geri

KICKS (continued)

Mae kekomi geri

Yoko geri

Ura mawashi geri

Kakato geri

Gyaku mae geri

Mawashi geri

Mawashi geri

Kakato geri

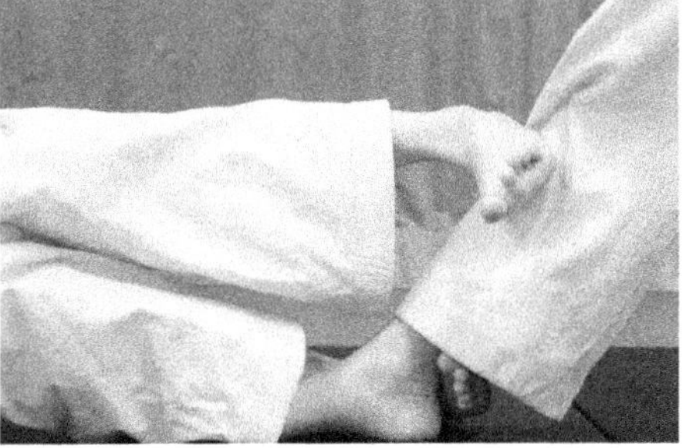

Yoko Kansetsu geri

"Karate aims to build character, improve human behavior, and cultivate modesty; It does not, however, guarantee it." - Yasuhiro Konishi

"Spirit first, technique second." - Gichin Funakoshi

THRUSTS

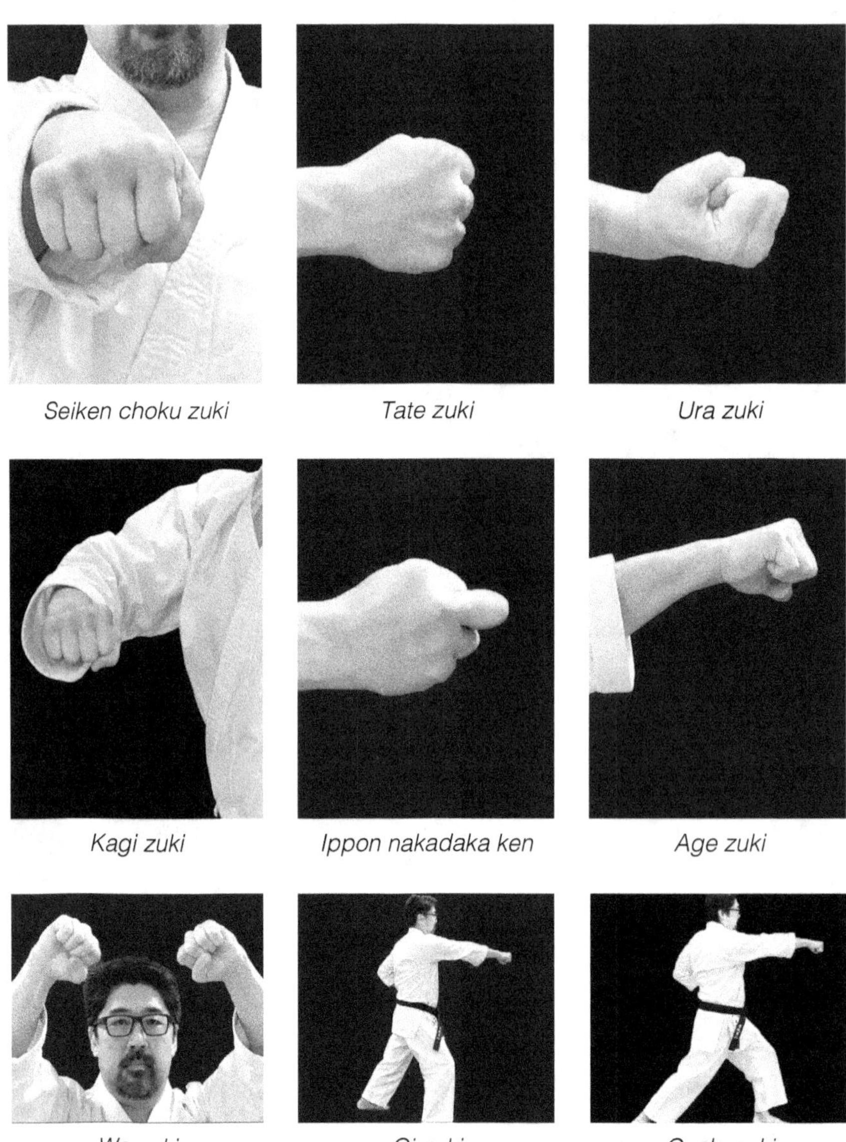

Seiken choku zuki

Tate zuki

Ura zuki

Kagi zuki

Ippon nakadaka ken

Age zuki

Wa zuki

Oi zuki

Gyakuzuki

"Tsuki," which translates to "thrust," is used in Karate and is quick, swift, and usually thrown in a straight line. The withdrawing fist, or "tsukidome," is also very important, while coordinated with the use of the hips.

THRUSTS (continued)

"Karate may be referred to as the conflict within yourself, or a life-long marathon which can be won only through self-discipline, hard training, and your own creative methods." - Shoshin Nagamine

KATA

Formal Exercise

Kata is formal exercise practiced in Karate which incorporates a series of movements designed to perfect form, agility, stamina, power, and speed. Studied and practiced properly, kata provides a method for creating and expressing various feelings and moods, and, at the same time, provides an excellent means to sharpen self-defense techniques. Kata also preserves various techniques created by masters from the past and present.

Perhaps most importantly, kata provides a path leading to spiritual-growth and understanding. This is so because through the continued practice of kata (and meditation), the mind and body begin acting as a unit. Wholeness and harmony are the result, and this provides greater strength to deal with the inner struggle of life. Kata is Karate's soul. It's also the backbone that shapes Karate's form, meaning, and beauty. It is the poetry of Karate-do.

Kata also lends physical expression to the words spoken above by Funakoshi, in that each kata begins and ends with a bow. If you keep an open mind, or the beginner's mind, this simple act should always serve as a reminder of the true essence of Karate-do which is striving to perfect one's character. Kata should be performed with spirit and strength, not arrogance.

A kata may have the quick, exciting, and beautiful movements of Wanshu (Excellent Wrist); the soft movements of Rohai (Vision of White Heron); or it may feature the bold, strong techniques such as those found in the Bassai (Penetrating Fortifications). There are more than 40 katas practiced in the Shito-ryu. And, while not all of them will become your favorite, each will be taught, and students should strive to learn them all. Eventually, after continued practice, you will gravitate to the katas which best meet your needs, desires, and capabilities. Those will become your favorites. You will also be encouraged to find the katas you most enjoy, however, you'll also be reminded to continue the practice of your other katas, as this is necessary to solidify your overall technique and skill. It is also necessary if, at some point, you desire to teach.

Serious kata practice will increase your agility, power, speed and flexibility.

Mastery of kata is essential because it helps fine tune a Karateka's body mechanics, including muscle memory, which is necessary to execute each technique properly.

Benefits

As you become older, kata training will increase because sparring and other contact exercise may become too extreme for the physical limitations that naturally accompany time. You will have already found kata a "way" to enjoy continued physical, mental, and spiritual growth.

One of kata's unique features is that you may practice anywhere, anytime. You don't need a large space, a partner, or any special equipment. The important point is to practice as often as possible. When angry or frustrated, kata practice will help you release your feelings and your thinking will become clearer and more focused. When calm and relaxed, kata practice will enhance your tranquility. When tired or lazy, the practice of kata will stimulate and refresh you. No matter how you feel physically or mentally, kata practice will fuel your growth.

Be Serious

Take your kata practice seriously. Whether in the dojo or home alone, you must focus intently upon what you are doing. It is fruitless to merely memorize a series of movements. You must understand that all the movements and techniques are interrelated, not random. You must explore and study. If you study and practice intently, you will understand this. And as you practice and grow you will begin to understand and appreciate the brilliance and beauty of each kata. When you gain understanding of your first kata, the second will become easier, and so it will be from then on with each succeeding kata.

Keep in mind that kata is many things, but first and foremost it is the backbone of Karate, and Karate is a system of self-defense. As you practice your kata, always picture an opponent in your path. Consider that you are practicing techniques that someday may save your life. If you're just interested in moving your arms and legs around, you should consider aerobics. You must be serious.

Line of Movement

When traveling, a map is used to chart the roads needed to reach your destination and to return home. In kata practice, basic "maps" are also present. They're called "lines of movement" or "embusen." These should be thoroughly understood so that you begin and end each kata in the same place. Failure to do so indicates that you have taken an incorrect step or that your stances were not uniform throughout the performance. Some of the embusen set forth in kata are the basic I and T, the straight line ______, and the cross (+) patterns.

The Kihon (basic) katas follow the I pattern. Naihanchi katas follow the straight line pattern. Bassai Dai follows the T pattern. Jutte follows the cross pattern.

Although changes have been made to include other angles of movement that may not directly follow the above lines of movement, the basic understanding of the core of the embusen will help you to understand and to perform each kata more precisely.

Multiple of Four

To practice kata for quick progress, do so in the "multiples of four" approach. The first time perform your kata slowly. Make certain that your movements and posture are as precise as possible. Difficult movements will require more attention. You may wish to extract those portions and practice them individually. The second time, perform the whole kata emphasizing power and "kiai," (spirit shout) points. The slower techniques should be done with proper relaxation and contraction of the muscles being used. The third time, emphasize speed while still maintaining maximum power. Lastly, perform the kata with normal speed, rhythm, power, and focus.

One day you may wish to create your own kata. At first, your creation will be based on logical reasoning and patterns, but you will notice that the kata tends to lose depth and becomes a mere physical exercise. It is only when you have gone beyond technique and have attained "Do," or the "Way," that you will be able to transmit that existence into a kata that will have deep meaning and character.

Tips to Improve Kata Performance
1. Wear a clean, pressed gi that fits well.
2. Announce your kata loudly and clearly.
3. Kiai with spirit.
4. Be certain to keep the tempo and rhythm correct.
5. Look sharply in the direction of each move before executing the next move.
6. Avoid appearing too stiff by relaxing and using full body language.
7. Know your kata thoroughly; prepare by practicing the multiple of four approach often.

PINAN NIDAN

Begin with the bow.

Announce the name of the kata and prepare.

Pull fists to sides and let rest in front of thighs with feet shoulder width apart.

Step to left cat stance and downward hammer-fist strike.

Step forward to right front stance and thrust.

Turn 180° to right front stance and block down.

PINAN NIDAN (continued)

Slide back to half front stance and execute hammer-fist strike.

Step forward to left front stance and thrust.

Turn 90° to left front stance and block down,

Step forward to half front stance and block upward.

Step forward and repeat.

Step forward and repeat with kiai.

Turn to back 45° to left front stance and down block.

Step forward to right front stance and thrust.

PINAN NIDAN (continued)

Turn to right 45° to right front stance and down block.

Step forward to left front stance and thrust.

Step to left front stance facing to the rear and down block.

Step to right front stance and thrust.

Step to left front stance and thrust.

Step to right front stance and thrust with kiai.

PINAN NIDAN (continued)

Step to left square stance facing 45° and left down open-hand block.

Step to right square stance and right open-hand block.

Step to right square stance facing 45° and right down open-hand block.

Step to left square stance and left open-hand block.

Return to shoulder wide stance.

End kata with proper bow.

PINAN NIDAN BUNKAI/OYO

"Kata without bunkai is like a shamisen (three-stringed traditional Japanese and Okinawan musical instrument); Nice sound, but empty on the inside."

– Choki Motobu (1870-1944)

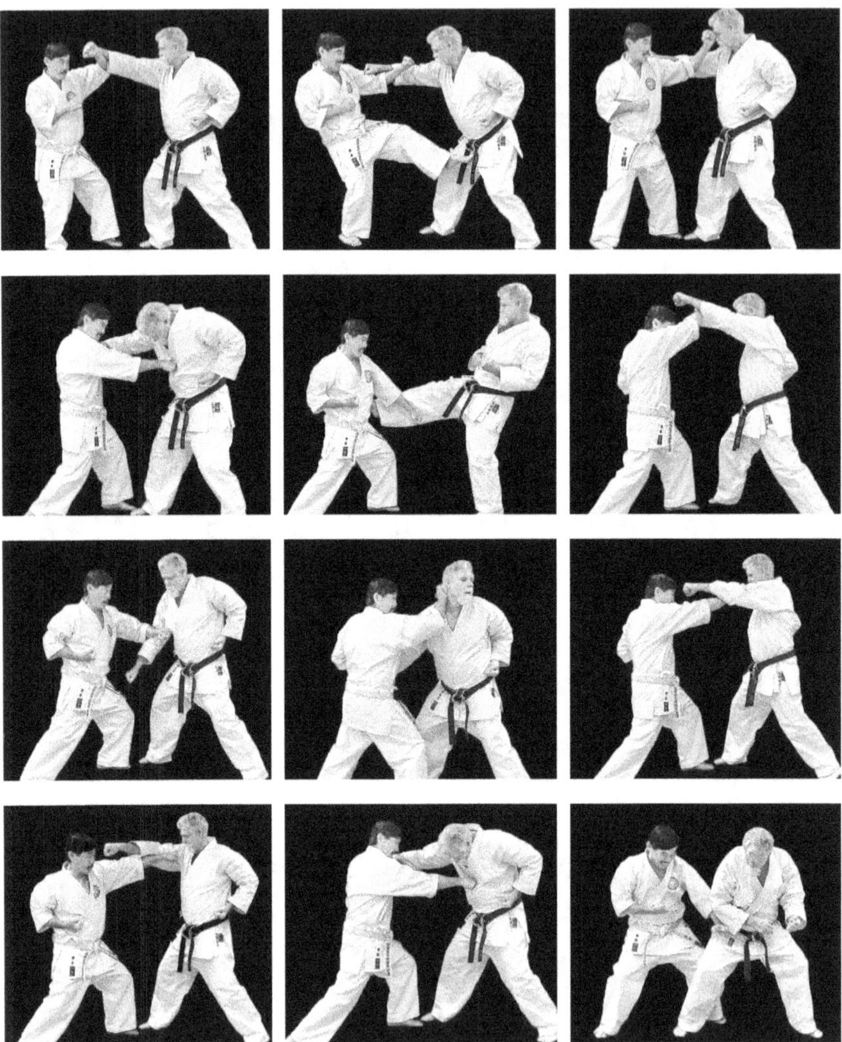

Bunkai is about analyzing and dissecting the kata movements; in other words breaking down each movement of the kata in order to apply it in a self-defense scenario.

Oyo is about the actual application of the analysis of the kata. If kata is to continue to exist, bunkai and oyo need to be understood and practiced regularly.

Initially students learn to apply the kata's movements against typical "Karate attacks," however as they become more mature, attacks should mimic a street fighter's approach; that is to be brutal, unconventional, and aggressive.

Students who faithfully practice bunkai and oyo understand the meaning of mutual cooperation and bring life to the practice of kata.

Kata Characteristics

Rohai

Wanshu

Bassai Dai

Annanko

JYU KUMITE

- Miyamoto Musashi

Free Sparring

Jyu kumite, or free sparring, is a method of training which gives students a chance to apply their techniques in a realistic fighting situation.

During Karate's early development, jyu kumite existed only in secrecy. The masters placed heavy emphasis on fundamentals and kata training. Sparring was restricted to the Yakusoku (prearranged) fashion. Not until the late 1920s did free sparring become openly introduced as a part of Karate training.

A Contradiction?

Undoubtedly, jyu kumite has become one of Karate's most controversial aspects. The average spectator must consider jyu kumite savage: Two opponents step quietly into a small square. They bow politely. Then, their sensei gives the command "Hajime," and the scene turns primal. Adrenaline flows; hands and feet fly. The combatants strike, kick, and scream. Each tries to land a decisive blow. At times the contest is decided in moments. Other times, when skills are even, the match is a prolonged, grueling test of individual will. Regardless, the scene is intense.

The common question is, "How does one justify the seemingly brutal and aggressive actions found in jyu kumite? After all, isn't the true purpose of Karate intended to lead to peace, harmony, and understanding, not violence and aggression?"

The answer lies in proper instruction and emphasis. Although seemingly brutal and aggressive, jyu kumite proves to be a useful tool in creating more controlled and passive attitudes among the participants.

As children grow up, their parents try to teach them all the important fundamentals necessary for them to become successful, happy, and well-balanced. Although a basic understanding of the fundamentals is present, it often does not penetrate deeply enough for them to fully understand. This comes only through experience. Similarly, sparring becomes a testing ground for both the physical and mental sides of our nature. In this way, through realistic confrontation, we come to understand the true nature of dualistic forces: positive vs. negative; hard vs. soft; active vs. passive; offensive vs. defensive; and so forth.

Instructor's Role

It's the critical role of each instructor to constantly promote and ensure the proper components of control, discipline, arid respect to their students during sparring. This lessens the chance of injuries, prevents negative attitudes, and brings kumite into a light of acceptance.

The weaker students leam to enjoy the many challenges of kumite and gain strength and confidence. Stronger students learn to have more understanding and compassion for their partners. In addition, they learn that brute force is not the answer. Rather, they strive to be more precise and seek perfection in technique.

"Mind Like Water" (Mizu no Kokoro)

When one finally masters the skills in kumite training, he will notice the overall calmness that exists even when the storm is great. Since techniques are polished, one's spirit is strong yet relaxed. You move only when necessary. You become aware of your opponent's motives and feelings and move accordingly when he moves. There is no concern for winning or losing, no antagonism toward your opponent, or any feeling of fear. You are in a state of "mizu no kokoro." You are able to calmly see and react to the true intentions of your opponent. Thinking about what to do is not necessary. Your "mind's eye" directs the proper offensive or defensive response. This is the ultimate goal of jyu kumite training.

Active and Passive

In order to achieve an advanced level of sparring where the response is accurate and automatic, one must use active and passive strategies. Active strategies may involve physical contact such as pushing, or pulling, or tactics that aren't physical such as a feint or a kiai. All distractions are designed to conceal your real intent and to break your opponent's physical and physiological balance. Break either, and you will control your opponent's actions. His mind and body have faltered and he is fighting himself to regain control. You now have the edge and opportunity.

Passive strategies use subtle body movement for distraction, or invite your opponent to strike you in a certain area by leaving the area obviously exposed. By doing so, you are setting up the conditions for contact and giving your opponent preconceived thoughts. Passive strategies attempt to make your opponent's mind labor over your real intent. If done properly, your opponent will become confused, uncertain, and will move incorrectly. He will expend useless energy while he attempts to regain his mental and physical balance. Thus, you are able to act in accordance with your opponent's weakness.

Sparring Practice

To bring together all the elements required for reaching the ultimate in free sparring, instructors use three types of training practices. These include the basic, semi-free, and advanced semi-free methods of sparring.

Basic Sparring: In basic sparring, one uses a predetermined offensive technique to strike his partner in a specified target area. This is done only upon the instructor's command. The partner receiving the strike will know exactly what technique is being used and where the target area is. He will attempt to successfully block the punch or kick and to counter-attack properly. Skills in stance, posture, timing, and distance are acquired in this manner. Students learn methods of attack as well as successful defensive skills. Students also learn the effectiveness of various blocks, strikes, kicks, grabbing, and throwing techniques.

Semi-Free Sparring: In this method, the attacker has a few seconds from the instructor's command to attack. He may use only a few specified techniques and must attack a specific target area. Prior to attacking, the attacker may use active and passive strategies. This gives the defender practice in using reflex motion, rather than just responding to the command and creates a higher level of physical and psychological skill.

Advanced Semi-Free Sparring: Here the attacker may use any one attack, using either hands or feet, to strike any allowed target area. Again, a few seconds are allowed after the given command before the attack must be initiated. As before, active and passive strategies may precede the attack. Because this is a more complex level of sparring, the defender learns to protect himself more completely. He also gains an understanding of how to respond more by instinct and intuition as opposed to calculation

Because this is the transitional stage to jyu kumite, it is critical that a serious attitude be maintained during the training period and that the highest level of fighting spirit is continually present.

Critical Elements

In jyu kumite training, your instructor will point out the essentials for continued success. These essential factors include the following:

Stance

Your stance should always permit movement in any direction. One of the most popular and effective stances is one where the feet are slightly more close together than they are in the forward stance The legs are bent slightly and the feet are neither too far apart, nor too close together. This stance enables you to move quickly and stabilizes your center of gravity, allowing more effective techniques.

Posture

The position of your body and arms often determines how your opponent designs his attack. If you're slightly crouched with your arms close to your body, your opponent may rush you and attempt to wrestle you to the ground. If your posture is more erect, your opponent may direct kicks to your lower body. Therefore, it is wise to maintain a well balanced posture. Keep your head straight and the front arm bent, with the fist about shoulder high and one foot in front of the shoulder. The elbow is tucked in to protect the side. The other arm should be placed so that the fist is positioned near the solar plexus level.

Eyes

Do not focus on your opponent's eyes. Although many instructors teach their students to look directly into the opponent's eyes, more success is found if you do not focus on any one part of your opponent's body. Rather, gaze as in meditating and see the whole body. Eliminate the guess work and place yourself in a physical and mental state that allows you to respond to your opponent's realistic actions.

Miyamoto Musashi, one of Japan's most famous samurai warriors known to the Japanese as "Kensei," or "Sword-Saint," summed up this notion well when he wrote:

"In strategy, fixing the eyes means gazing at the man's heart... In single combat you must not fix the eyes on details. As I said before, if you fix your eyes on details and neglect important things, your spirit will become bewildered, and victory will escape you. Research this principle well and train diligently."

Distance and Space

The distance you maintain from your opponent is a crucial element of sparring, and in determining the outcome of the match. You must know your strengths and weaknesses as well as those of your opponent. This analysis determines the proper distance to maintain. You must be prepared. If an opponent enters your zone or space you must either move back instantly to maintain your space, or you must counterattack. If all other factors are perfect, but you have misjudged the distance, your error will be costly. Not only will you miss your target, but you will be vulnerable to a counterattack.

Timing

To take advantage of an opening created by either you or your opponent, you must have the correct timing. To move too soon or too late will cause you to become physically and, perhaps, psychologically off balance. Again, your opponent will have the opportunity to take advantage of your carelessness. The time to initiate an attack is:

1. When your opponent is changing his stance from one side to another. He is often off balance at this moment.
2. When your opponent initiates an attack. Here you are creating and taking advantage of the psychological imbalance which occurs when the opponent is thinking so firmly about being on the offensive that his defensive reactions are slowed.
3. When your opponent feints. The element of surprise comes into effect and an opening is created for you.
4. Right after your opponent exhausts his initial attack. Attack immediately. Don't allow him time to reorganize his thoughts.
5. When your opponent loses his fighting spirit. Once spirit is lost, the opponent can be pressured to respond to almost anything, making your attacks very effective.
6. When your opponent is between exhaling and inhaling. (Refer to the section on kyo.)

After many hours of jyu kumite practice your timing will improve, and you will be able to respond to your opponent's actions more creatively and effectively.

Practice until your mind and body work in unison, and your actions and reactions will become instinctive.

Will and Confidence

If you are to attack successfully the instant an opening appears in your opponent's defense, you must have will and confidence. Most opeings exist only for a moment. If you hesitate, the moment is lost. You must have the will to act. And you must have confidence in your techniques. If confidence is absent, your will to act carries the heavy burden of emotions like fear, anger, and uncertainty.

The only way to elevate confidence is through proper and consistent training. Practice until mind and body work in unison and your actions and reactions are instinctive.

Control

This refers to both physical and mental control. Your instructor will constantly remind you of control.

Physical control is a fine line. Your goal in sparring is to land a decisive blow. Yet, you must never injure your opponent. To stop your blow three inches from your opponent's head is no good, but to make severe contact with the head is far worse. Your blow must be delivered with power, speed, proper form, and focus. You must control your technique to the head to connect with just skin touch.

Contact with certain target areas of body is allowed, but again, control is required. During practice, you will learn to make light to moderate contact with these targets which will enable you to feel your strikes more thoroughly. A degree of contact is also helpful in strengthening the bodies of those, receiving the blow. You must remember, however, that each student is unique. A blow that one opponent may barely feel might injure a weaker opponent. Students must concentrate.

By constantly practicing this contact-control concept, you will understand the difference between too much control and excessive contact.

Occasionally there is the rare, insecure student who seems to enjoy making excessive contact. If, unfortunately, you are of this type, do not expect instructors not to notice or care. They will.

You must also control your feelings and emotions and not let the egotistical attitude of winning or losing prevail. Many students lose their cool when they feel that their partner is getting the best of them, only to find themselves at a greater disadvantage. You must stay calm and train with the proper attitude.

Talking

Talking, is a practice best avoided during sparring. Words are fine, functional, and useful, but like everything else, they have their time and place. When actually sparring, just spar. Let the body feel and learn. Let the mouth rest. Often, when a higher ranking student feels that a lower ranking student is getting the better of him, the senior student will want to stop, talk, theorize, and point out the numerous deficiencies in the lower ranking student's technique. This is a shallow ploy. Your techniques improve through practice, not unnecessary discussions.

In all areas of training, including jyu kumite, students of all ages need to be first taught about respect, discipline, control, and focus.

If your attacks are to be successful, you must have will and confidence.

KYO AND KUMITE

Often, even from well trained Karate students, we hear such remarks as, "I knew he was coming, but I couldn't do anything about it. He was just too fast for me."

Or, you'll hear someone say, "I can't figure it out; I just didn't see him coming." What do these comments really mean?

We all know there are times when the attack, be it a punch, kick, or strike penetrates right through the defense. But, there are also times when the opponent seems to know exactly when the attack is coming and can easily stop the attacker, even those with the best speed and technique. Does this mean that our hope of survival is a mere 50-50 chance?

We are often told - with certain mystical overtones - that one can, with sufficient training, know exactly when the opponent will strike. And, therefore, he can respond with the appropriate counterattack. What is this source of knowledge? Is it an intuitive or instinctive response? Can it be reduced to theoretical knowledge, which may then be used in practical application?

Sources of Knowledge

When climbing the mountain of training and research, one finds three basic sources of knowledge: the teachings of martial arts masters, samurai combat tales, and through personal study and experimentation.

Knowledge can be acquired by observing a real master who embodies both knowledge and ability. A good teacher will emphasize the important principles of attack: striking just before the opponent makes his move for attack; striking at the same time the opponent attacks; striking just after the opponent has attacked; and creating your own opening in your opponent's defense, then striking.

The implications of these principles are enormous. To be accomplished in kumite, one must not only know the moves of his opponent, he must also be able to block accurately so that he can make the opponent respond to his will. But the ability to actually get this done remains a mystery or an impossibility to those who limit their training to only the above principles.

The second source of knowledge is found in the samurai combat tales and includes both written and verbal stories which transmit hints and suggestions. These stories contain frequent references to the expression "kyo o tsuku" or, "kyo o tsukareru." Kyo is variously translated to mean "void," "non-substance," "empty," or, in this context, "an unguarded moment" or "an opening." Thus, "kyo o tsuku" can be translated as "strike at the kyo."

Kyo is also found in another context. This is in the phrase used in and out of Karate dojos, "Myo wa kyo-jitsu no kan ni ari." One professor of Buddhism translated it as, "Profundity is found between the non-substantial and substantial." This reflects profound, mystical thought, but it would seem difficult to relate it to Karate.

Use of these two knowledge sources is helpful, but they still do not fully enable us to know the moment before the opponent strikes. And, explanations of kyo as an "unguarded moment" or "opening" are good but not sufficient to allow us to know exactly when such moments occur.

The third source of knowledge is that of personal study and experimentation with the possibilities and limitations of the body. Aside from considering an individual's ability to master the concepts or the technical movements, studying and experimenting with combat leads one to recognize two critically important factors that determine the success or failure of the outcome. These factors are timing and distance. The study of proper timing returns us to the question of when the opponent will strike, or when you should strike. Note: The study of distance is also crucial. If your attack or your opponent's attack does not reach the target, there is no contest.

Breathing

In our examination of the various limitations impeding the mastery of technical movements, (and factoring in the importance of timing and distance), brings us to the discovery of the role of breathing. This is a fundamental yet crucial component in Karate practice. Our knowledge of the importance of proper breathing technique and the vital role of the breath during movement, tends to remain in the shadows of human awareness. Both the physiology and the psychology of breathing must be studied and understood.

Studies show at most, we can make only four or five strenuous movements without breathing, and there is a rhythm in our breathing that determines and governs all our movements. It is impossible to have strong physical focus while inhaling. These studies tell us that we can only strike or block strongly when we exhale. Since we cannot move well without oxygen, we have to inhale before we can execute a strongly focused attack.

It now becomes apparent that if we can focus our attention on the breathing rhythm of the opponent, we clearly know when he will strike. He can block or strike strongly only if he has inhaled. While he can inhale as he moves, he is almost helpless at the point when exhalation changes into inhalation.

The meaning of "kyo" now becomes clear. Kyo means "emptiness." And the phrase, "Myo wa kyo-jitsu no kan ni ari" can now be understood to mean, "Mystery is found between emptiness and fullness," that is, between exhalation and inhalation.

Startle Reflex

If we understand the physical limitation that breathing imposes, especially at the point of exhaling, we can then exploit it. This can be done through the so called "startle reflex." Our instinctive reflex when startled is to inhale. In Karate, we can be startled by a sudden change in attention through visual perception (seeing), auditory perception (hearing), and tactile perception (touch). This explains why quick, short jabs to the face, a loud shout, a quick touch to the opponent's forearm, or stomping the foot before a major attack are useful tools of combat. While many students use these techniques randomly, they can be used consciously and deliberately to make the opponent react, either by creating an opening or by making him counterattack. In other words, you're forcing your opponent into a state of kyo. Once the reaction is known, one can choose to strike immediately or to await the counterattack so that a strike can be made immediately after it, during the pause between exhaling and inhaling.

Theoretical knowledge and practical application are two different things. Understanding when you should strike, or when your opponent is likely to strike, and of how to create an opening so that you may strike, is helpful. But, it takes years of training to internalize this knowledge and use it instinctively. Those who have trained for years but are still experiencing the same problems and questions mentioned at the beginning of this section would do well to remember, "Myo wa kyo-jitsu no kan ni ari," (or the secret lies between exhaling and inhaling).

More can be said about breathing and alertness, even consciousness. However, this must remain the subject of the individual student's research.

Strive to understand and perfect the basics of sparring. Not only will you become proficient in defending yourself against an attacker, but you'll also begin to deal more proficiently with life itself.

"No matter how you excel in the art of "Ti" (precursor to karate), and in your scholastic endeavors, nothing is more important than your behavior and humanity as observed in daily life." - Junsoku Uekata

WEAPONS

Although Karate is an art that basically doesn't use weapons, the customary practice of combining the unarmed and armed martial arts techniques in China influenced the remainder of the martial arts world. Many of the weapons, such as the "nunchaku," "tonfa," and "sai" can be traced to Chinese origins. The "bo" (six-foot staff) or "kon" (meaning staff in Chinese) and the "kama" (sickle) are probably weapons incorporated into martial arts directly by the Okinawans.

Because metal was scarce and arms were banned, the use of these unobtrusive farming and fishing tools as weapons developed rapidly. And because the people of the Ryukyus led simple, peaceful lives, their overlords never suspected that the Okinawans had cleverly turned the use of these basic daily tools into a means of self-protection and a high art form.

Several weapon katas are practiced in Shito-ryu. (A list of these katas is found in the Appendix on page 127).

Many of the weapons used can be traced to China, but their applications demonstrate Okinawan characteristics.

Tonfa

Kobudō training is part of Saito-ha Shito-ryu's curriculum.

Sai

Eku

Bo

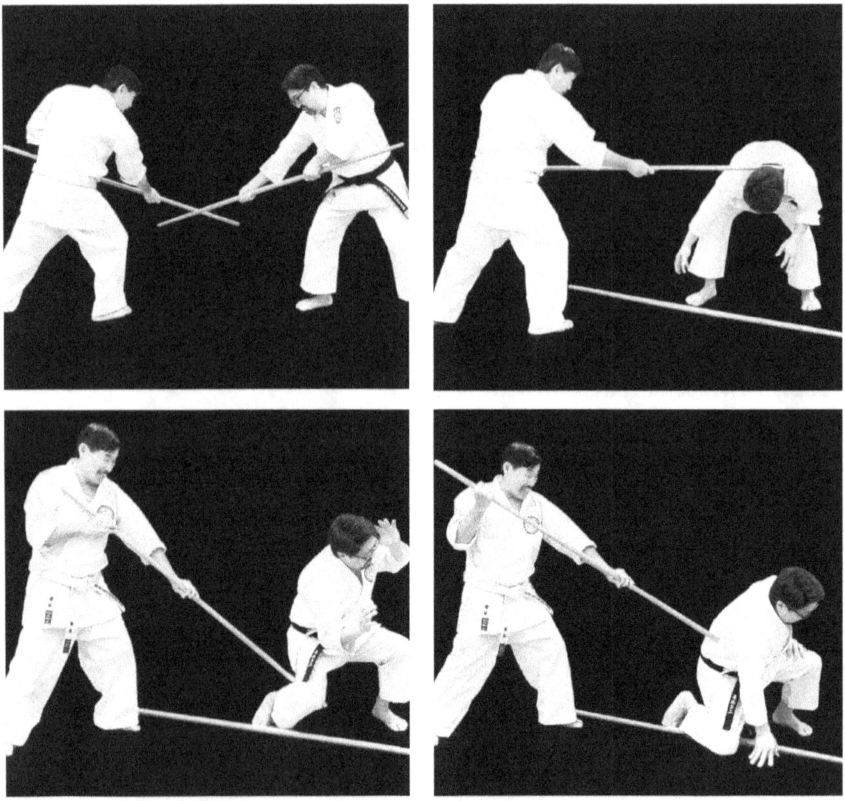

Nunchaku

TAMESHIWARI

Karate training includes "tameshiwari" which are techniques used in breaking boards, rocks, ice, and other materials. Some students join Karate schools hoping that they will be able to smash through several boards with their hands or feet. They eagerly seek the "magic" which allows such powerful feats without causing injury or pain. Yet, there is no magic involved, and tameshiwari is far more than a trick.

Smashing the Negative

Tameshiwari offers another excellent example of how the dojo becomes a microcosm of the world beyond its doors. In it we find a parallel to the dualism constantly confronting us in our lives. Most of us, on a daily basis, face instances where half our mind tells us we can do something, and the other half argues that we'll just fail or make fools of ourselves.

Many students stand before the boards and tell themselves they can smash them to splinters. Then, full of confidence, they fire a mighty punch. But in the brief instant it takes the punch to reach the board, the mind fires a negative message: "It's going to hurt; the boards won't break; you'll look like an idiot." And before fist meets board, fear of pain and failure sap the punch of its pure energy. The results are the same in everyday life when the mind whispers its negative tune, and nagging doubts creep in. Energy split into different directions is diluted. The negative wins. The board remains unbroken; the only thing splintered is the spirit.

Negative thoughts are, perhaps, the toughest thing in the world to break. Instructors do not associate tameshiwari with brute strength. They teach that hard work breeds strong technique which breeds confidence. And when technique is clean and the mind is calm, students do, indeed, smash the boards. More importantly, they learn that they can smash the negative thought process.

Tameshiwari also teaches students just how dangerous their techniques can be if used ungoverned by proper attitudes. It is of utmost importance that students practice tameshiwari only under the close supervision of a qualified instructor.

Condition your hands and feet properly before attempting tameshiwari.

TOURNAMENT COMPETITION

Those seeking a high level of competition will enjoy participating in tournaments. Some of these contests will be small affairs with only two or three dojos participating. Others will be large and draw competitors from throughout the nation, and even from foreign countries. These larger tournaments allow you to test your skill against some of the world's most talented Karate-kas.

Winning and Losing

The record shows that our students consistently perform well in major competitions and have won many medals in state, national, international championships. And while tournament trophies and titles are important, instructors realize these are external symbols, and instead place a much higher value on the internal victory. They teach that winning has little value if not graced with humility. They also teach that there is great reward in losing if one gains in experience, confidence, and spirit.

Some schools lack depth and stress only winning. This one dimensional approach is ultimately a weak one. If one wins, then boasts and brags, strutting arounds, he actually loses. If one loses a match, yet acts with dignity while learning, growing, and sharing good spirit, he wins. Striving to perfect one's character has a much deeper and more enduring value than any trophy or title.

Karate tournaments feature kata, kumite, and kobudo types of competition.

Kata

The individual kata match is the most popular in kata competition. Here the contestant performs his favorite kata before a panel, usually composed of five or seven judges. The kata performance is similar to the gymnast's routine. The gymnast tries to creatively combine grace, power, and fluidity while flawlessly demonstrating each movement. The kata performer strives to do exactly the same.

The individual kata match is based on a point system, or flag judgement. After a contestant completes his kata, each judge displays his decision with a score or flag. The contestant receiving the highest point total or unanimous flag tally at the end of the competition wins.

Competition provides students the opportunity to test their skills.

An "uramawashi geri' is very effective and worth three points.

Kumite

Kumite competition includes individual and team matches. Individual matches generally last two to three minutes. Two contestants pair off (one contestant is designated "aka" or red by means of a red belt, and the other is designated "ao" or blue by wearing a blue belt) in a ring that measures eight meters square. The contestants are matched based on a combination of factors which may include age, experience, height, and weight. The panel refereeing and scoring each match consists of one referee ("shushin"), and four corner judges ("fukushin"). A time keeper and score keeper are also present.

The matches are based on an eight-point spread system. This means that within the time frame of the match, the first contestant to score eight points ahead of his opponent's score is declared the winner. If time expires before a contestant has scored the maximum points, the match is awarded to the contestant ahead on points. A referee awards the points as either a "yuko" (effective thrusts or strikes), "wazaari" (effective kicks to the body), and "ippon" (effective kicks to the head), or a take-down, followed by an effective technique. Proper form, correct attitude, vigorous application, "zanshin" (continuation of strong spirit), proper timing and correct distance must all be present in the technique for an score to be awarded.

During kumite matches, attacks are limited to the head, face, neck, abdomen, chest, and back (excluding the top of the shoulders). Excessive contact with the allowed target areas, or contact with areas such as the groin, will result in a penalty. Contestants will be disqualified for using profanity or any other unsportsmanlike conduct.

Team matches are generally conducted with five members per team. The contest is the same as individual matches, except the winner is determined by the total number of victories claimed by a team.

Victory is always sweet, but to win over yourself in defeat is priceless.

Free sparring gives students a chance to apply their techniques in a more realistic fighting situation.

Although seemingly brutal and aggressive, kumite leads to controlled and passive attitudes.

KARATE AND PHYSICAL FITNESS

"Men are born soft and supple;
dead, they are stiff and hard.
Plants are born tender and pliant;
dead, they are brittle and dry.
Thus whoever is stiff and inflexible
is a disciple of death.
Whoever is soft and yielding
is a disciple of life.
The hard and stiff will be broken.
The soft and supple will prevail."

- Lao Tzu

Endurance and physical fitness are essential in Karate training. A well performed kata demands superb coordination and stamina. Wear down quickly in kumite, and you'll be at your opponent's mercy.

Primal man survived through physical effort. Constant activity made him strong; constant danger made him aware. He needed no additional fitness exercises.

Modern man is sedentary, surviving primarily through cognitive skill or by performing dull, repetitious activities, and neither contribute such to physical fitness. The average person today spends far too much time watching instead of doing and driving instead of walking. Little time is allowed for physical activity.

Modern man is a victim of the soft, physically protected, overindulgent, emotionally stressful, affluent society he has created. By 30, advanced aging effects from sedentary living and untamed appetites have produced various "modern" diseases. These include obesity, chronic back pain, weak abdominal muscles, low endurance, hypertension, ulcers, and headaches. Many are quickly victimized by depression and emotional instability. It's little wonder that a number of students begin Karate as eager participants only to find themselves totally exhausted after just one hour of activity. Excuses begin to become more prominent as students find themselves unable to withstand the physical demands training presents, and they begin to try to find ways to avoid class.

Until recent years, the epitome of physical fitness was characterized by a "Mr. Universe" physique (to some extent this notion is creeping-back into acceptance today). The more bulging the muscles and the more weight one could lift, the more one was thought to idealize the concept of ultimate physical fitness.

Form Follows Function

Experts now focus on endurance and stamina as the true measure of physical fitness. Stamina is the amount of time a muscle, or muscle group, can perform at or near maximum capacity. These two vital functions are the crux of the body's ability to meet the demands of performing kata, kumite, or, perhaps, in dealing with an unexpected assault.

Two components are required to achieve the level of fitness necessary to succeed in Karate and perform the techniques effectively. First, the cardiovascular system must be finely tuned. In other words, your heart and arteries must be able to withstand the vigorous activities Karate requires. Second, the body must have a flexible musculature system that is firm and defined, allowing supple movement and rhythmic endurance. Bulging muscles actually restrict fluidity, and conversely, soft body lacking tone will not be able to meet the physical demands.

If you're convinced that physical fitness is mandatory to reach high levels of Karate performance and understanding, you may already have questions as to what form of exercise program is best suited for you. Since the actual practice you receive in class cannot be concentrated merely on physical fitness, it is extremely important that you make time each day to practice and exercise on your own.

After loosening up and stretching with the exercises learned from your sensei, practice on the basics, making certain that each technique is performed as accurately as possible. Kata practice should follow. Perform each kata using the (multiples of four approach) as explained in the kata section.

You may wish to follow your kata practice with more sit-ups and stretching exercises, or by striking the punching bag. Always allow the body time to cool down gradually. Don't stop exercising abruptly. In the last five to ten minutes of your workout, slow your movements. Proper stretching cannot be over-emphasized. Build in time at the end of your practice for stretching. Complete each session with meditation and, if possible, a refreshing shower.

As your endurance and stamina begin to develop, your next task is to maintain this fitness program. This is more difficult, but to continue for only a few weeks or months will produce only mediocre benefits. You must continue your program throughout your life. Maintain your efforts, and you'll find your power, speed, coordination, and endurance will improve greatly, and this will only enhance your Karate performance. You'll also discover that you look and feel better in your daily life. You'll reap the benefits of the added energy and confidence that a sound physical fitness program provides.

SELF-DEFENSE FOR WOMEN

Observing nature, we see that predators single out and attack the weak, the young, and the old. It is the same in human society. Human predators look for signs of weakness and insecurity in their victims - a "sure thing." And to the predators, who are mostly male, females look like easy marks.

For the woman who studies Karate howeever, the would-be assailant makes several faulty assumptions. He believes that since he is a male, he is physically superior simply because he is bigger (and probably stronger) than his intended target. Relying on this presumed advantage, the male thinks he can easily control and victimize the female. However, as pointed out earlier, brute strength and force are of little or no value in Karate. The elements that count are a blend of form, balance, speed, focus, timing and distance. These elements, properly combined, produce strong technique and powerful strikes and kicks. If physical strength does not play a role, then the male's primary advantage, at least as he perceives it, is negated. Therefore, the male who assumes he can easily subdue any females is committing a serious error in this instance.

Practicing Karate dramatically increases your chance of surviving an attack. No matter how big or strong the assailant, his anatomy presents many vulnerable areas such as the eyes, nose, throat, solar plexus, groin, and knees. You will be trained to take advantage of these weak spots. If you train properly for a period of time, panic and fear won't consume you when confronted by an attacker. Instead, your mind will be centered, and you will focus on the techniques and skills needed to successfully defend yourself. Remember, if you're ever attacked, your assailant has already underestimated you. This is to your advantage.

Every situation differs, so it cannot be pre-determined which techniques are the best to use. That would only be misleading information. The important thing to remember is that when you decide to make your move you must be decisive and accurate. Do not stop until you are certain that your attacker is too disabled to harm or pursue you.

Naturally, it is best to try and avoid an attack in the first place. Usually, you are more susceptible to being victimized when you are in a hurry and forgetful, or when you become careless of the possible dangers lurking in society. There are steps you can take to make yourself less vulnerable. Karate practice will constantly remind you of the dangers around you and will add to your awareness. The following are few reminders to help insure your safety:

At Home

Protect your door with a strong frame, sturdy hinges, a chain latch, and a strong deadbolt lock. Make certain yor door has a peephole.

List your first initial rather than your first name on your mailbox, and when providing your contact information. Do the same for mailing lists and monthly billing and bank statements: for any mail coming to your residence.

Always check through the peephole before opening the door.

When talking on the telephone, never reveal personal information about yourself to any stranger.

Don't give reason for a peeping Tom to hang around your home. Close blinds, curtains or drapes at night for added privacy.

Keep in mind that the majority of women assaulted are not victimized by strangers, but by someone they know.

On the Street

Carry your purse with a solid grip, and keep it close to your body.

When shopping, never leave your purse in a shopping cart, on a counter, or in a dressing room.

Walk in the middle of the sidewalk, away from doorways and cars that could conceal an attacker.

Avoid taking shortcuts through alleys and deserted parks, especially at night.

Whenever you're in contact with the general public, whether in person or on social media, avoid wearing suggestive clothing. Be aware of the type of attention you're seeking, as you can never be sure how the way you are portraying yourself will be interpreted.

At Work

Keep your purse in a locked desk drawer or file cabinet. If you use a cloakroom or locker, do not leave your keys and other valuables in your coat pockets. Keep them on your body.

If you must work late, alert the building custodian or a trusted co-worker and ask him to meet you in the lobby to walk you to your car when you leave.

Leisure Time

It is best not to go out alone at night unless it is absolutely necessary. Safety exists in numbers.

Don't invite trouble by going to bars and nightclubs alone.

Go for walks in parks or other secluded areas only during daylight hours, and take a friend along.

In Your Car

Have your keys ready when you get to your car so you won't have to spend time searching for them.

Remember to activate your car alarm every time you leave it.

Lock your doors as you leave it during the day, at night, and always when driving. Lock your doors when you are sitting in your car.

Before you unlock the door from the outside, look in the windows and check the front and back floors to make certain you don't have any unwanted passengers.

Make certain that you have enough fuel to get to your destination.

Travel busy, well-lighted streets as much as possible. Avoid driving in the curb lane at night.

If your car breaks down in an isolated area, raise the hood and sit inside with the doors locked until help comes. Don't open the windows or unlock the doors to talk to strangers offering assistance. Instead, ask them to call the police for you.

If you have an automatic garage door opener in your car, hide it out of plain sight. If a thief breaks into your car and sees the opener, chances are good he'll also find your vehicle registration, and the next place he'll show up is at your home, automatic opener in hand.

Always refuse to pick up hitchhikers - no matter what the circumstances.

Precautionary measures such as these may save your life.

Awareness

Again observing nature, we see that animals in the wild never take their environment for granted. Those that do often die young. Those that grow to old age are constantly aware of their surroundings. Sadly, most human beings pay scant attention to their environment, preferring to believe in the false notion that really bad things only happen to other people. This is one of the worst mistakes you can make.

Keep in mind that the ultimate goal in self-defense is to avoid harm, and that defending yourself is not limited to punching and kicking. You must do whatever it takes without pause: shout, bite, scratch, or run. Purchase and carry a whistle, pepper spray, or hornet-wasp spray. If you are aware, impromptu weapons are usually available. Learn to identify and use them: a purse, umbrella, rock, stick, your keys, or shoe can be used to keep an attacker at bay. Even sand or dirt can be useful in protecting yourself. If you're attacked, matters become deadly serious. It's not what is pretty or fair that counts but whatever it takes to save yourself from harm. Your instructor will work with you on this and stress ways to increase your awareness.

Practice

You might wish to practice various attack situations based on normal, everyday activities. Your instructor can arrange this form of practice for you. If you desire to conduct this type of practice in street clothes, that is fine. First you will learn to defend yourself adequately against an attack by one assailant, and then, gradually, you'll learn the proper measures to take if attacked by more than one person. You must practice sincerely and consistently.

Striking the nose with the palm heel of the hand, and a knee kick to the groin can prove very effective.

After the Attack

It would only be normal to be nervous if attacked. Nevertheless, try to memorize all you can about the attacker including his weight, height, race, hair color, features, eye color, clothing, and jewelry. If they speed away in a vehicle, memorize the license plates, color, and make of car. You may be able to only get part of this description, but any information you can provide authorities will be beneficial in leading to an arrest and conviction of your attacker.

If you become the victim of a rapist, don't keep it to yourself. That is destructive to your well being. Share the incident with someone you respect and trust, seek counseling, or both. Inform the authorities at once and try to cooperate. It may be an unpleasant experience, but try to be patient and calm. Getting your assailant off the street and behind bars may save countless women from your fate - or worse. Whatever the circumstances, remember, people can sometimes succeed in attacking your body, but they can never attack your mind - unless you let them.

Assailant grabs from rear.

Extend arms and push hips backwards.

Heel kick to groin.

Assailant grabs around neck.

Step to side and backfist to face.

Strike groin area.

Extend arms and wrap around elbow.

Force him down by pushing down on arm.

Pull and turn him on his back.

Control his arm.

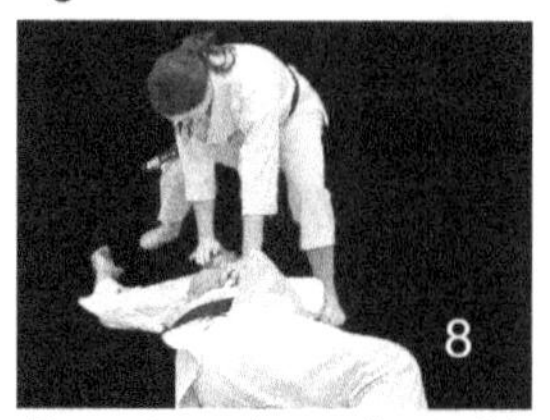

Execute palm strike to his nose.

Assailant grabs lapel.

Place hands on his wrist and firmly push down.

While maintaining control, kick his groin.

Continue to control his arm.

Push his arm firmly downward.

Keep his arm against your shoulder and maintain pressure on his arm.

Assailant places hands on shoulder.

Look towards him and stand tall.

Control his arm by keeping it straight.

Strike with a full-scissors strike to throat.

Place right foot behind his leg.

Push him while sweeping his leg from
under him and palm strike to his jaw.

Assailant approaches you from back.

And wraps your arms.

Reach up and grasp the upper arm.

Strike the leg with a hammer-fist strike.

Elbow strike to the ribs.

Grab the upper arm again and place your hip close to assailant's hip and leg.

Throw assailant over your hip.

While still securing assailant's arm, strike the jaw using your palm.

Elbow strikes are very effective to include in your self-defense arsenal.

Advanced Techniques

Assailant applies a headlock.

Control his left arm.

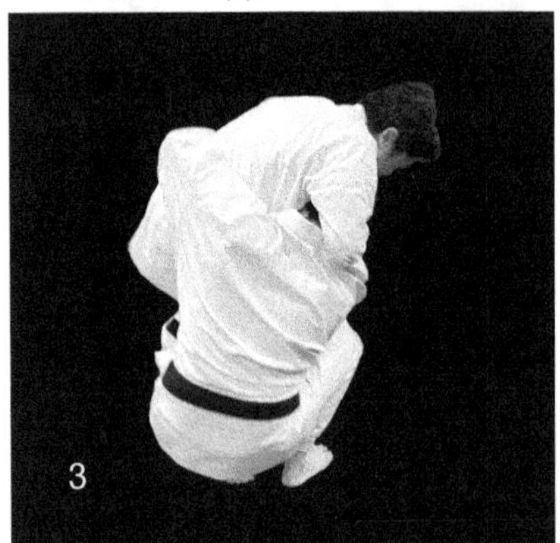

Grasp his left side with your left hand.

Roll him on his side,

Secure his right arm with your neck while grasping your wrist.

Maintain pressure on his neck and arm.

Advanced Techniques (continued)

Slip your arms upward toward his elbow.

Straighten your body and turn inward to place more pressure on his arm.

Assailant grabs you from behind.

Lift both of your arms upward.

Lift arms high as possible.

Execute elbow strike to his ribs.

Advanced Techniques (continued)

Wrap your right arm around his arm.

Crouch, pull and throw him over your shoulder using your legs and hips.

Maintain control of his arm and kick his elbow area with your shin bone.

Finish your technique with a thrust to his jaw.

Dip low to avoid punch to face and thrust to a vulnerable target.

Place right hand near ankle and left hand by knee area. Pull and push to topple your assailant.

Maintain control of his leg.

And quickly thrust to his groin area.

As assailant attacks you, drop to ground and quickly execute a round kick.

Hook and pull his left foot with your left foot, and push his inside left knee area with your right foot.

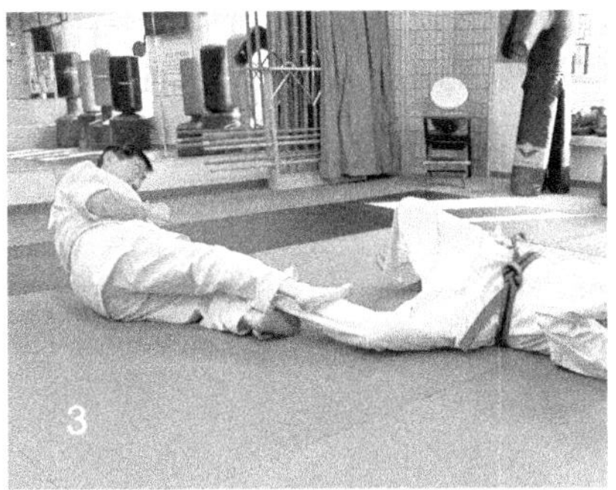

As he falls down, slide your body closer to his.

And follow through with a kick to his groin.

Advanced Techniques Cont.

Prepare to be attacked.

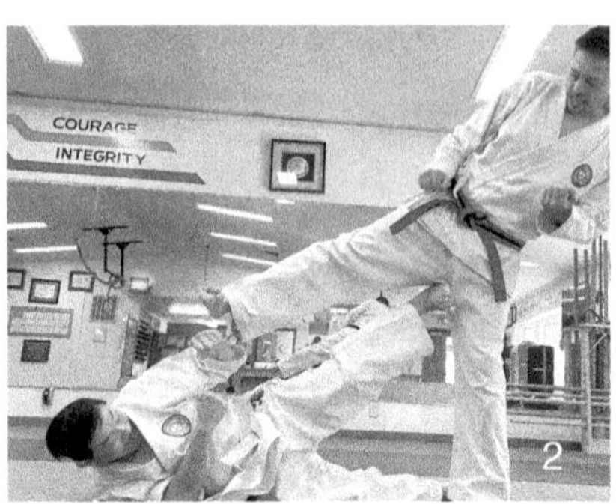

As assailant kicks you, drop quickly and side kick to his groin.

When attacked, quickly move forward and strike to throat.

Apply an elbow restraining technique.

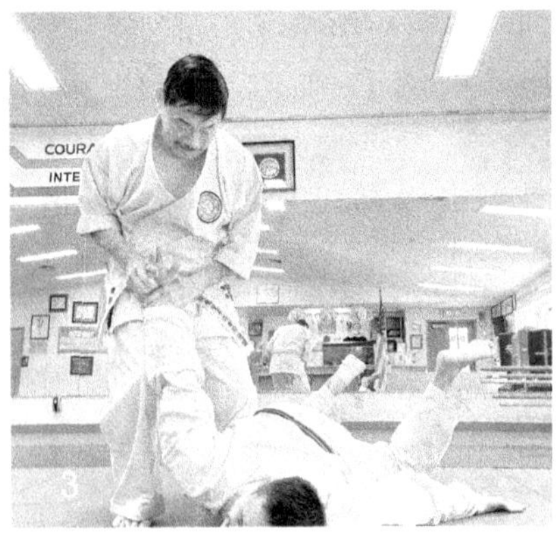

Continue to place pressure on his elbow and wrist.

Apply inside pressure on his arm with your legs and drop your left knee on his shoulder blade.

KARATE-DO IN DAILY LIFE

"The mass of men lead lives of quiet desperation."
                                                        - Thoreau

Thoreau's observation is probably more accurate today than when he first expressed it roughly 150 years ago. We live in the freest society on earth, yet many of us feel like prisoners caught in a technological age we cannot fathom.

We are a consumer society, and our society is being consumed. Little is left to hold onto as we slip closer to the edge. Drugs numb the mind. Television sells "reality" while stealing the soul. We've trampled our traditions to dust; we burn the American flag, and for the life of us, we can't decide what is moral.

The average marriage falls apart faster than a new car. We shove the elderly into "communities" or the "old folks home" at the first opportunity. The average attention span has been reduced to the length of a TV commercial. Schools become ineffectual as academic proficiency scores plummet each year. Discipline, manners, and respect for others have been scrapped like old clothing, and we embrace the latest therapy theories and the "hottest" new assertiveness training programs. Many children are left to "do their own thing," or are simply ignored, and as a result they are left adrift.

We waste our nation's resources then seek to take from other nations that which is not ours. Most people show little respect for our environment. Nature is something to be cut, cleared, and conquered, drilled, pumped, developed, and sold. We have set ourselves apart from and above nature, and have become totally out of step with her rhythms.

Greed is the operative word as we sell our country off piecemeal to the highest bidder, and the meaning of life has been reduced to bumper-slicker mentality: "He who dies with the most toys, wins." In other words, he who has the most possessions is most blessed.

In all areas of life we have learned to accept the lowest common denominator. The slogan, "Made in America" was once a source of great pride. Now, as our industry parallels the decline of our society, that slogan has become a joke at best, a warning at worst.

These are the seeds we have sown, and our harvest is bitter: unable to make a difference, we become indifferent; unable to accept, we reject; unable to understand, we blame; unable to love, we hate. Never have so many seemed so determined to extinguish the last flicker of inner light.

From this abyss, Karate-do provides a moral path, a life-long road leading to enlightenment and understanding. Any martial art which only values and teaches just physical techniques adds little to the individual student and serves to further disrupt and threaten society. Karate-do, however, emphasizes physical, mental, and spiritual unity. It is a quest for a higher moral and spiritual plane. Karate-do provides a unique vision; the world is seen with more compassion and sensitivity. Daily life is, therefore, approached with greater serenity and kindness.

Formality, respect, tradition, and discipline are the cornerstones of any good dojo. And, to a degree, the dojo reflects the world in which we live. In it we meet people from all walks of life, and each person appears different from you and me; our backgrounds, goals, likes and dislikes differ. Yet, as we study and train, gaining internal and external strength, we begin to see that at the core our needs are the same: not one person exists who does not need food to nourish the body. Likewise, not one person exists who does not need respect, kindness, compassion, and understanding to nourish his soul and spirit. This is true regardless of age, sex, size, race, or physical appearance. We understand the truth of this not just in the dojo but in our daily lives, as well.

Through practice and training we learn many things. We discover that Karate-do is not just confined to the dojo, to tournament victories or trophies, or to defending against an attacker on the street. Katas - as all katas begin and end with defensive moves - teach us the meaning of, "Karate ni sente nashi," which translates as, "In Karate, one does not make the first strike." And, just as we learn to block punches, strikes, and kicks, we learn to block the angry words and provocative gestures of our fellow men.

As we conduct our personal lives, we know that strength has nothing to do with winning fights or forcing our will on others. True strength lies in the ability to stand firm to our moral commitments. When it is necessary to let irritants pass, we are able to do so. If it is best to walk away from foolish confrontations, we walk away confidently, without remorse or hesitation. We also possess the courage to meet any adversity or crisis with great resolve and capability.

As we follow the spiritual path of the "do," our approach to life becomes quieter, more respectful. And, as we discover more about ourselves, we discover more about our true place in the universe. Ultimately, it becomes clear that there's but one significant victory in life - the victory over one's self. With this understanding life's important values - harmonizing with nature and our fellow men - become clearly focused and embraced. The rest is smoke and shadow.

PROMOTIONS

The Early Days

Long ago, in Karate's early days, a student received only one belt when he first began practicing. It was white. Students cherished these belts and wore them with pride. Gradually, after many hours of practice, the belt began to show age. Little-by-little, the belt became increasingly dark, reflecting the passage of time and the student's effort. The belts natural coloration was the only indication of student "promotion."

Not until Jigoro Kano, the founder of judo, adopted a promotion system for his art did Karate incorporate the basic ideas for a colored-belt promotion system. This symbolic representation of the various stages of progress vary from school to school.

Today

As a rule of thumb, the approximate time spent at each level, from 10th kyu to 4th kyu, is two to four months per level, which equals about two years of training. An additional 16 months of training is usually required to pass the exams from 3rd kyu to "Shodan-ho," or the provisional black belt rank.

Black Belts

The Shodan-ho ranking places a student in a one-year probationary period. During this time, the student wears the black belt but is not officially recognized as a Shodan, or first-degree black belt, until the probationary period passes. Throughout this time, the shodan-ho must continue to train in good faith and live in accordance with the principals of Karate-do.

From Shodan on, technical skills in all areas remain important. However, promotions are actually based more on the individual's character and contributions to the art of Karate-do.

Many students expend great effort to reach the shodan-ho ranking only to quit training shortly thereafter. This is unfortunate, because although their techniques have sharpened their minds have not. Such students believe they have reached the end of their journey, received their "degree," and are ready to move on. The fact is that Shodan-ho is not where learning ends but where it begins. It's not like graduating from college but is more akin to graduating from high school. This is a critical juncture where a basic understanding and adaptation of Karate-do finally become a reality. From this point, one begins to use that reality to form and create a life of much deeper substance. Earning a black belt only to quit, is like getting married one day and divorced the next. One can make many excuses, but they will show no wisdom. There are wiser ways than making excuses.

Polish the Character

T.S. Eliot said that, "Our exploration shall never cease. And the end of our exploration will bring us to the beginning, and we will know the place for the first time." So it is with a worthy promotion system.

All students are urged to seek promotions. At the same time, it's urged that students receiving a higher rank do not relate to the color of their belt. To think of yourself as a brown belt and someone else as "only" a blue belt is narrow thinking and not the true "way" in Karate-do practice. This is similar to thinking, "I have to spar an opponent, but I'm big and he's small, so I'm going to win." Wisdom lies not in focusing on the color of belt but in the mastery of technique and the polishing of character.

If a student fails a promotion, it is urged that he talk with his instructor to review areas of deficiency. When one is able to meet failure with a positive outlook and as a possible stepping stone for future growth, he will be inwardly and outwardly worthy of attaining each successive rank.

Senior students must avoid using their rank to take advantage of subordinate students. Students must practice humility and set a fine example for others to follow. Only with full cooperation and with the most wholesome attitudes can promotions aid in maintaining the high qualities and potential of Karate-do.

This fine parable may help you understand the difference between two men as they received higher levels of promotion:

A student asked his sensei, "What is the difference between the little man and the man of 'do?' They both seem equally proficient, yet you see things otherwise?"

The sensei replied, "Someday you will begin to understand, but I will tell you this much. When the little man receives his first dan, he can hardly wait to go home and tell everyone on his street of his accomplishment. Upon receiving his second dan, he will climb the roof top and shout his promotion to everyone. Then, when he receives his third dan, he will hire a limousine to parade him through the street with banners telling everyone he has made third dan."

The sensei continued, "when the man of 'do' receives his first dan he will bow his head with gratitude. When he receives his second dan, he will bow his head and his shoulders. Then, when he re-ceives his third dan, he will bow to the waist and quietly walk among the people, not to be noticed."

THOUGHTS FOR INSTRUCTORS

*"All people have the spirit - it is just a matter of
careful guidance. It is just like jade in the
matrix - if you throw it away, it is just a rock,
but if you cut and polish it, it is a gem."*

\- Gaoan

Good instructors walk a fine line. Many students entering your dojo will, for the first time in their lives, be in an environment governed by tradition, respect, formality, and discipline. These elements are fundamental to your dojo and must guide your actions. Yet if the atmosphere is overly strict and rigid, you'll find this is self-defeating. The key is in balance. Here are a few things all instructors can do to achieve that balance and also strengthen their ability to teach more capably, thoroughly, and accurately.

Just as parents guide and direct their children to ensure healthy growth, you must do the same with your students. To accomplish this, you must have the desire to teach and have the proper attitude at all times. Having these critical prerequisites, instructors will find themselves constantly striving to improve their own skills. Obviously, instructors pursuing their own growth will greatly enrich their students' abilities to grasp the intricacies of Karate. Students will notice the added energy and confidence in their instructors and will respond with a surge of positive, flowing energy. Training will be extremely rewarding when this occurs.

For students to grasp the underlying morality of Karate-do, discipline, etiquette, and principles must be an integral part of the program. This is the delicate area where balance must be achieved. The instructor who comes across as a remote, cold drill sergeant running a regimented boot camp will fail. Many students, especially the younger ones, will quickly quit such a program and enroll in any of the numerous upbeat and entertaining exercise programs offered today. Do not overplay Eastern cultures and traditions. Wholesome two-way communication is minimized when other cultures are over emphasized. This results in misunderstandings.

It is especially important in the beginning and intermediate classes to create an environment that is firm, yet yielding. Strive to make these training programs enjoyable. Remember, the beginning of any venture is usually the most tentative stage. Students at this level are more insecure and unsure of themselves. Although they may be learning techniques and katas, they haven't had the time necessary to absorb the deeper meaning and purpose of Karate. You must be patient, kind, understanding, and, most of all, encouraging. Students respect instructors who bring these qualities to their teaching, and you'll find your students willing to accept firm guidance.

This is not to say that instructors should not strive to bring these same qualities to their advanced classes and students. Variation, stimulation, and enjoyment are keys to any good teaching program. But as your students increasingly advance and begin to grasp the broader picture and deeper significance of Karate-do, the harder they will be willing to work and discipline themselves to arrive at each successive plateau. Nevertheless students, no matter what the rank, are human beings first, and, as such, need encouragement, respect, and kindness.

Training with other instructors is an excellent way to improve your technical skills, and teaching skills. Training together in a special session once a month shouldn't be too difficult to arrange. By training together, instructors can share ideas, problems, or any pertinent matter necessary to strengthen themselves and their personal growth. This type of training also creates a sense of community that is vital to the organization.

Instructors who make no effort to train together use the excuse that because they are actively teaching, they do not have to train. The end result of this is that students drop out when they discover their instructor's teaching lacks depth. Worse, injuries may occur more frequently, especially when students become stronger and more developed. Instructors who do not train usually have to prove their abilities in an unprofessional manner to retain a semblance of respect from their students. Their own lack of control and confidence is readily seen by the students. When such instructors are threatened in sparring, what control they do have is lost and injuries result.

Good instructors do not cater to their stronger students just to improve their dojo's tournament records. Wise instructors understand the needs of all their students, including those who need delicate attention. The good instructors will give these students the extra encouragement and support they need. Talking to students on a one-to-one basis is an excellent way for instructors to learn the true personalities of their students and determine their inner needs. This individual contact also enables instructors to structure their classes in a manner which better meets the needs of the students.

Concentrating all the training and activities strictly within the dojo is discouraged. Instructors must learn to expand the dojo activities to areas outside the dojo. This could include occasional beach training, picnics, camping trips, and other outside activities. By having novel activities, students begin to realize that their instructor doesn't regard them as mere clients.

By extending the boundaries, students realize the instructor is extending his feelings and concern to them. As this occurs, students act in accord and show greater care and respect for their instructor. These activities also promote greater friendship among the students and lead to mutual support and encouragement. This spirit adds vitality to their Karate training.

Other methods to strengthen your teaching and make your classes more dynamic may include the following:

1. Invite guest speakers to discuss or demonstrate subjects as First Aid, diet, nutrition, other martial art styles, or police science.
2. Have another instructor sit in on one of your classes and critique you on your teaching format.
3. Present demonstrations with your students at the various schools, clubs, and shopping centers in the area.
4. Use video equipment to more accurately show students their performances.
5. Have periodic informal discussions with students.
6. Have your students write haiku (a form of Japanese poetry) or a research paper on any worthy topic and then share it with the other students.
7. To create greater values, friendship, and unity, have your students elect officers to initiate periodic meetings for the entire dojo membership.

At times, instructors will be confronted with students facing financial burdens who are unable to pay for classes. In such cases, it is necessary to consider the facts that have created the situation. If the student cannot pay for classes because he chose to purchase a new television or wardrobe, then he must be told to budget more wisely and to return to classes when he has the finances to pay for his instruction.

In some cases, instructors will find that a student wishes to train or to continue training, but cannot pay for his instruction because of unexpected events or tragedies. I suggest that the student be given some work to do at the dojo or at the instructor's home, or perhaps the student could perform some type of community service in return for his lessons. Students will be extremely grateful for the understanding, and for the opportunity to continue training. Their gratitude will be evident in their magnified spirit during training. The rewards will manifest themselves in many ways.

Splitting wood for an elderly citizen is a good way to offset the cost for tuition.

Helping a young mother by carrying her baby while she trains.

Lil' Dragons classes gives senior students the opportunity to teach.

COMMUNITY SERVICE

Taking part in and supporting the Annual Polar Plunge to benefit the Special Olympics.

Assisting our local Law Enforcement Officers sharpen their self defense skills.

DEL SAITO — A JOURNEY OF WISDOM
By Jose M. Fraguas

He is one of the most highly respected Karate-do instructors and officials in the world. His expertise in the art of Karate has made a great impact not only in the United States but also beyond the American frontier. Born and raised in Hawaii, Del Saito began his martial arts training at the age of 11. He received his Karate training from two of the most outstanding instructors in the Shito Ryu style, Chuzo Kotaka Sensei and Soke Mabuni Kenzo, son and heir of the great Mabuni Kenwa.

More than three decades of teaching Karate has led to a strong traditional approach, combined with an openness to new ideas and concepts for growth. Teaching Karate for more than technique, he attempts to help people to find themselves, to discover their creativity and their capacity for overall growth through the arts of Budo. His goal never has been to glorify himself, but rather to preserve all the knowledge passed down to him by his teachers in order to perpetuate the art of Karate.

As the past National Executive Director for the AAU Karate, Hanshi Del Saito believes that a moral and ethical base should be taught in all the dojos: "Karate is a system with deep traditional roots. Our spiritual needs, our morality, and our beliefs have slipped into an abyss," he says. "It is important to act to involve ourselves with proper attitudes and to find out more about the absolute truth. This is the true basis of the art of Karate-do."

How long have you been practicing the martial arts and why did you start Karate training?

"Back in my childhood, I watched a lot of Chambara (samurai) movies, but Karate and other martial arts were still mysterious to me. I knew more about sword fighting than any other martial art. My introduction to martial arts as a practitioner came when I was eleven years old, in 1961. I had convinced my parents to sign me up for Judo in Kahuku, a nearby sugar plantation town, and I can still remember the vigorous formal exercises that we were put through, as the sound and smell of the sugar mill also were a part of the dojo. I was just a skinny kid and many of my partners were on the chubby side and had a few pounds advantage over me.

I hadn't yet figured out the throwing techniques and depended a lot on strength, which I also lacked. Needless to say, I cleaned the mat on many occasions and would go home frustrated. I wouldn't dare complain, however, because I knew my dad would lecture me on commitment and not feel sorry for me one bit. After a year of that "abuse," I was fortunate to meet Sensei Al Kahalekulu. He introduced himself to several of us kids during our summer break and asked if we were interested in Karate. I jumped at that opportunity and managed to talk my parents into letting me sign up for his classes. As I recall, I told my parents that tuition was only five dollars per month and that the dojo was only a couple of miles away from home, in Sunset Beach. They agreed and a happy kid emerged from a shaky start in Judo to a more tolerable art of Chito-ryu Karate-do.

What was most interesting or challenging to you as a youngster?

In Karate, I would have to say that it was how to break boards and cinder blocks. My friends and I would meet after school or on the weekends to challenge each other on who could break the most boards or bricks. We would constantly be toughening our hands and feet by striking hard rubber targets or jury-rigged makiwara pads. Our knuckles would get all callused and that was our trademark for Karate excellence. No one would mess with you if you had those calluses. Fortunately for me, that period did not last for more than a few months. The pain we suffered when the board or brick proved harder gave us a lot of laughs as well as tears.

Aside from Karate, sand surfing had a great appeal to me. As the waves would swipe the sand and leave a slick surface, I would run, throw my flat smooth board in front of me, and jump on it for a thrilling ride into the oncoming surf. If my timing was less than perfect, the board would stick in the sand or would be enjoying the ride without a rider.

For lessons in life, the most interesting as well as challenging thing would have to be the Christian education I was exposed to since I was five years old. My parents were leaning towards the Buddhist religion back then, but never hesitated in placing me in a Christian School. We were taught strict principles and our teachers and pastor would even frown upon dancing. Yet the biblical stories and lessons were interesting and made a lot of sense. A lot of positive seeds were planted in my mind in those early years, and it was always a challenge to stay on the straight and narrow path. I can say, though, that a sound spiritual base has been vital in steering me through much stormy weather and many of life's challenges.

How many styles of Karate or other martial arts methods have you trained in?

Kodokan Judo, Chito-ryu Karate-do, Shito-ryu Karate-do, and Muso Jikiden Eishin-ryu Iaijutsu.

Who were your teachers during all these years?

I had several. When I met Sensei Palimo (Judo), I was only eleven and don't remember too much about him, other than his emphasis on mat work, proper methods of grappling, footwork, throwing, and submission techniques. Later he allowed randori (sparring) and I certainly had my share of being an easy uke for the more advanced students.

Al Kahalekulu Sensei was a gentle yet tough sensei and he was the saving grace for me to exit from judo training. He introduced Karate to me, and for that I will always be grateful. His training was tough and he always reminded us to polish our character. He made his monthly home visits to check how we were behaving and was a big asset for our parents, as they could keep us in check when we would get a bit testy. His Chito-ryu instructions helped me develop confidence. Interestingly enough, as I got better, he would use me as an uke and I found judo once again.

Chuzo Kotaka Sensei was my first Shito-ryu instructor. He emphasized the kihons and that in itself solidified my overall Karate foundation. His version of Shito-ryu was a modified one which incorporated many shotokan movements. I managed to learn his explosive type of front kick that I still depend on until this day. His vision was directed more into competition, and many of us did quite well in that arena. He still maintains that competition focus and his students continue to be very successful, winning at all levels of competition.

Kenzo Mabuni Soke was my second Shito-ryu instructor and I came to know him as a sincere and good man, a friend, and a sensei who wanted to pass on his father's legacy as best he could. He had a clear vision as to what he wanted to accomplish. He wasn't interested in subjecting me to doing things exactly as he had his students do in Japan. Rather, while instructing me in kihon, kata, and kumite, he would point out things that Seito Shito-ryu emphasized. One of the major differences from his ryu-ha and my last Shito-ryu experience was keeping all the preparatory positions closer and less exaggerated. Once I accomplished this, he was very pleased, and I was very happy to finally learn a more purer version of Shito-ryu.

Masayuki Shimabukuro Sensei was my Iaijutsu teacher. I was always fascinated with his stories of the samurai, their strict code, and their ability to use the sword. Shimabukuro Sensei has helped me understand how to make the sword come alive through perfection of technique and spirit.

What was your first impression of Al Kahalekulu?

A very powerful man who you did not want to mess with. Yet, you could sense compassion and kindness that kept one from avoiding him. Sensei Kahalekulu was a big Hawaiian man whose arms were larger than both of my thighs, and yet he could move very quickly and gracefully, which really impressed me. He taught me many lessons on life and his encouragement made it possible for me to improve my leadership skills. In the dojo, he would bark out commands, and because he gained our utmost respect, we poured everything we had in every class. In those days, we could not even scratch an itch or look around while we were in training. If you did anything that was unacceptable, a quick sting of the shinai reminded you to maintain total awareness on the task at hand. Our dojo was in an old house that someone had let us use, and the screenless windows invited many mosquitoes that we used as our excuse for getting swatted by the shinai. After each class, our dogi would be soaked from the workout, and walking home afterward in the cool offshore breeze made everything worthwhile.

Have there been times when you felt fear in your training?

I never felt fear in my training but needed lots of encouragement in teaching classes. I was very shy and had difficulty getting in front of people. The Karate environment changed all that, as no one teased or commented negatively when I first began assisting in class. Unlike giving a book report in school, everyone in the dojo was respectful and understanding.

What did your father do for a living?

My dad was a carpenter and worked for my uncle Fred Shimote for many years. He then joined the union and began to work on some larger projects like the Del Webb Kuilima Hotel, now the Turtle Bay Hilton, on the North Shore of Oahu. My parents were born on Maui and were second-generation Japanese. During summers of my younger years, my dad would take me to work with him and would teach me how not to hit my thumbs with a hammer. I learned how a finish carpenter had to have lots of patience and carpentry skills to produce a finished product with excellence.

Who were some of the Karate notables when you first began Karate training?

Well, there were quite a few names that I kept hearing back then, the first being Dr. Tsuyoshi Chitose, the Grandmaster and founder of the Chito-ryu Karate-do group, who had his headquarters in Kumamoto City, Japan. Then there was Sensei Tommy Morita, who was the chief instructor of that style in Hawaii. I also would hear about other instructors, whom I eventually met later, such as Sensei Bobby Lowe of the Kyokushinkai group, Walter Nishioka from the Statewide Karate League, James Miyaji from the Butokukai, Kenneth Funakoshi from the Shotokan group, and Chuzo Kotaka from the IKF, whom I eventually trained with. There also were other instructors in other disciplines that were heading strong organizations in Hawaii as well as on the mainland, such as Professor Okazaki, a massage therapist and Jujitsu expert, Professor William Chow from the Kempo group, and Sonny and Adrian Emperado of the Kajukenbo group. As there were many ethnic groups in Hawaii, so were there diverse Karate styles. This led to a strong martial arts base that eventually would make a great impact for the growth of Karate in the United States as well as abroad.

In the late sixties and early seventies, I was fortunate to meet several influential instructors who helped expose Karate to many people throughout the country, if not throughout the world. One of them was Ray Dalke Sensei. He was one of the top JKA American instructors who trained directly under Hidetaka Nishiyama. I came to know Ray as a friend and respected him for his courage to accept me, a non-JKA (shotokan) practitioner, as his peer, rather than his adversary. We would practice together and help each other with the tournaments we held. About that same period, I was introduced to Sensei Dan Ivan. I remember him as a considerate, kind, and very knowledgeable martial artist. He shared his interesting stories while he lived in Japan. He always helped me arrange demonstrations for my tournaments with his popular Japanese Village demonstration team. He reminded me of David Krieger, who helped Kotaka Sensei establish the International Karate Federation. Dan did the same for Sensei Fumio Demura, as they established the Japan Karate Federation in this country.

It was about 1971 that I met Sensei Chuzo Kotaka, and after several meetings, he accepted me into his organization. He impressed me with his strong techniques and beautiful form. He appointed me National Director for the IKF and I carried that position until 1999, when I decided to establish my own organization.

It was also in the 1970s that I met Sensei David Krieger. He was an exceptional man with a gentle heart. His Karate was good, and we had lots of great times together, both in Hawaii and in Santa Barbara, where he presently resides.

Why do you think you and your friends were able to keep out of trouble?

Many of us were poor compared to those who lived in the city. Parents lived paycheck to paycheck, and that taught us to share, to be creative, and to enjoy the outdoors. We all had gardens to manage and from that came many of our meals. We learned to work together and oftentimes we would all congregate at one of our buddies' homes to help him finish his chores in order for him to play with us. Most of the moms were at home, and they all made sure we behaved. Whenever anyone of us failed to measure up to what was expected of us, our parents were informed, and the belts didn't feel so good when our dads came home. Parents also took the time to teach us skills and lessons in life. They made sure we addressed the adults as Mr., Mrs., Miss, and Sir or "Uncle and "Aunty," even if you were not related to them. Whenever we made a promise, they made sure we followed through. We also had supper together and I think that kept a tight family. We would never want to do anything that would shame our families or let our parents down.

How long did it take you to really "get" Karate?

Not until many years of study of not only its technical aspect but also the challenges that solidified my understanding of character. The mental training was very trying and difficult to accept at times, but after hours of repetition, things started to connect and made sense. The clarity of the philosophy at times would become very cloudy, but that was because the underlying agendas of the Karate leaders made it almost impossible to grasp the full concept of this art. Interestingly, the politics, personal goals, and organizational strategies of the leaders had a great deal of influence on the standards of Karate. Some organizations were like fraternities, and if you endured their initiation and oftentimes humiliation, then you were considered one of the boys. Many traditional instructors prohibited their students from learning from other instructors and would ostracize those who did. It was all of those kinds of things that caused me to understand Karate-do, and it was from then on that I felt it was my mission to help maintain Karate-do in the spirit it was meant to be.

What was your biggest frustration in training?

From the technical point of view, at first the movements were very foreign, and it took many months of training for them to sink in. In my early days of training, I was unable to reference books, video, or television. Everything was totally new, and many aspects of Karate were missing. It was like putting a puzzle together with many of the pieces missing. However, through time, I began to understand the principles that allowed me to execute the movements properly without being too stiff or overly zealous to be the best in my class.

The dojos of yesteryear usually were at community centers, churches, or classrooms shared by other groups, and supervised training was limited to only a few days per week. I wanted more direct instructions from the sensei, especially in the beginning stages, and I was frustrated when formal training was limited to only a few hours per week. My biggest frustration, however, was due to instructors who thought that their style was the only one that had any merit. Their tunnel vision caused many students to eventually abandon the traditional styles and to form their own open or "eclectic" styles. Perhaps that trend would have occurred anyway, but I would argue that it was because of these earlier instructor's attitudes that Karate was revolutionized in this country.

Another frustration is how many instructors still hang onto the coattails of past martial artists who seem to have no one equal or better. If all that they still advocate and teach holds true, why is it that no one has yet achieved such a level of excellence. I know that in my style of Karate, we have many outstanding teachers, students, and athletes. Even my students now have surpassed me in many areas, and I am grateful that I was able to teach them.

Are any of the students you grew up with still active in Karate?

I don't think so, not from the original group of guys and gals that started with me. However, a good friend, John Isabelo, who began training with me a few years later, trained with Sensei Walter Nishioka in Honolulu. He earned a Medal of Valor while serving with the Honolulu Police Department and was one of their outstanding homicide detectives. He retired from the Honolulu Police Department and later served as an investigator for the Attorney General's office for the State of Hawaii. He presently conducts classes for our organization in Hawaii

Who were your biggest role models?

Definitely it would be my mom and dad. Clara and Toshio were loving and kind parents and always taught me life skills that I have learned and accepted. Mom was a housewife and always was home to care for me and my five brothers. She was always washing clothes, sewing, or cooking, and kept everyone in line. We had to learn how to wash, cook, iron, and clean house. My dad was a carpenter and worked constantly. Even after returning from his job, he would be working in the garden or doing something that he managed to involve us in. We would do everything the old-fashioned way, which was never easy, and he made sure that we did it right. He would even make his own bows and arrows and I would be the one to turn the handle for his makeshift lathe. I sure did my share of grumbling, but little did I realize at that time that dad was teaching me how not to be afraid of work, which would have positive results both outwardly as well as inwardly. He was also an accomplished skin-diver and taught me how to spear fish. He also showed us how to play the shakuhachi (bamboo flute). I must say it was one of the most difficult musical instrument for me to get a reasonable tone.

My dad was interned right after the attack on Pearl Harbor. He was placed in a camp at Tule Lake, California, for about four years. Eventually, I began to ask my dad all kinds of questions about his ordeal, which I thought was totally unfair. He never once had anything negative to say about our country, even though he had to endure those troubling times. He would remind me however, that in order to prove that we (the Japanese people in Hawaii) are good citizens, we needed to move on to become productive and hard workers. I always remembered those words of wisdom and respected him even more.

Aside from my parents, my first instructor had a lot of influence on me. His concern on my well-being also helped me at home. Sensei Kahalekulu would make periodic visits to my home and would check to see if I was practicing my Karate, by-laws, and resolutions. My parents also would remind me, whenever I became too testy, that their report to sensei would not be taken favorably. I would immediately straighten up, as even the slightest thought of upsetting him was too shameful.

I attended Sunset Beach Christian School on the North Shore of Oahu from kindergarten to eighth grade. One of my favorite teachers was Miss Aileen Miller. She was a sweet educator who had lots of patience, and her love for her students was very apparent. Her close relationship to the Lord, total commitment to her mission work and daily instructions, provided me with an abundance of hope in the years of challenges that would come my way.

David Krieger was another great man whom I admired, and was in many ways a role model for me. He was well-educated and the person responsible for getting the IKF started with Kotaka Sensei. He held a Ph.D. in Political Science and headed the Peace Now Foundation (a nuclear disarmament program) based out of Santa Barbara, California. Since then, he has also completed law school and obtained his real estate broker's license. He also is a very accomplished Shito-ryu sensei and founded the Pacific Karate-do Institute. David Krieger was a gentle man who would find good in people and did not dwell on the negative. Although very intellectual, he would not even remotely talk down to anyone, even if they were quite ignorant. I admired all he stood for.

Another role model was my late friend, Mr. Henry Takaki. He was the local postman and would take time on the weekends to gather a few of us kids to treat us to a movie. He would teach us how to communicate and think and would do so by cleverly asking us things that would spark our interest. He always was involved with community organizations and spent countless hours in keeping the North Shore community alive and educated. He was instrumental in guiding me to be involved with community projects and taught me about volunteerism.

Did you prefer kata or kumite?

I preferred kumite at first because we were not allowed to spar until several months after signing up for classes. We would watch the adults spar and then, on the way home from the dojo, stop at Ehukai Park at the Bansai Pipeline and mimic the moves. We made sparring very dramatic as we would announce to our opponents what technique we were about to do. As I recall, the "Shooting Star" was one of our favorites; it was a glorified jump kick that was prepped by Kung Fu-like hand gestures. We had a blast and thought that was the ultimate in Karate. It was not until my senior year in high school that I became more interested in kata. I guess I came to realize that the kata held more information and learning tools that I could gather with more acceptance and seriousness of its practice. That realization came from my personal development and maturing. As I'm getting older, I enjoy kata more than ever. The bunkai-oyo, or practical application, and kakushite (hidden techniques) are fascinating, and the wealth of information kata holds always amazes me. I still enjoy kumite as well, as it pushes me to maintain my agility and stamina while maintaining my distance and timing practice. It also is more enjoyable sparring with my friends as we have come to learn how to train with it rather than to prove our strength by hurting each other.

Did you compete a lot in Hawaii?

Not a lot. When I first started training, my instructor was not into competition. It was not until the late 60s that I began to compete in Hawaii, and I competed in only a handful of events there. By the seventies, I had already moved to Southern California and was more interested in preparing my students for competition. The last tournament that I competed in was in Hawaii in the early 80s, where I was fortunate to win first in all my events.

Most of the tournaments I competed in were in California. Kumite in those days were all "shobu-ippon," or "one-point" matches. You could be preparing for a tournament for months only to be beaten in a couple of seconds. There were only a few round-robin or double elimination tournaments. And repechage was not even heard of. Athletes back then did not want to win by contact penalties, either. If your nose was broken, you would hold the bleeding with toilet paper and be ready to fight on. We were tough then but perhaps our young impressionable age made us a bit foolish. But how much fun it was just to survive. I just hope that the abuse we put our bodies through doesn't come back to haunt us.

The most enjoyable and memorable competitions and events were those at the Japanese Village and Deer Park presented by Senseis Fumio Demura and Dan Ivan. Not only was the Japanese Park setting ideal, but there were always players from Japan who kept the competition interesting. One year, after winning the Black Belt Kata division, I met a stocky Japanese in the finals. After several exchanges, I landed a front kick to his stomach that nearly tore my toes off. He just stood there and did not show any signs of pain until a few seconds later. The pain was excruciating but the win made it bearable. Until this day, I am reminded of that match every time I look at my crooked toe.

Who were your greatest rivals and what were they like?

I guess I would have to say the players from Japan. In those days, all you heard about in competition was how tough the Japanese Nationals were. They were the ones that ruled. So whenever I had the opportunity to face one of them, I was very prepared. Fortunately, I was able to beat every one of them. Aside from competition, our greatest rivals were the students and instructors from other dojos. Oftentimes, they would appear unannounced to challenge you to a kumite match just to test your worthiness. Some of those fights would get pretty rough, but if you emerged victorious, you would be left alone. Those that didn't fare well eventually closed their dojos.

What are your favorite techniques?

I have managed very well with keeping my arsenal simple. I rely on foot sweeps, thrusts and front kicks for success. The magic is in the timing, distancing, and confident execution of the techniques; and of course, strategy has an important role in packaging my delivery. Some have said that I have a mean look about me when I'm in the ring which causes my opponents to be intimidated. If that works, I guess I won't be needing the services of a plastic surgeon.

How has your personal expression Karate developed over the years?
One of the positive changes I see is that more traditionalists are allowing their students to mingle and to train with other instructors in the form of clinics. It would seem a given that an instructor would see to it that his students have accomplished instructors. As an example, parents who think they can teach their children everything, and not allow them to be exposed to others to be taught or mentored, are surely stunting their potential to grow. As for development of the Karateka, I believe today's students are stronger, have more technical savvy and develop quicker than those when I first began training. The understanding of nutrition, stretching, muscle development, psychology, plyometrics, et cetera, plus easy access to information, gives the modern Karate warrior access to many more pieces of this fascinating puzzle. Of course, the old timers who are still active also have progressed and can hold their own. They still possess courage and confidence that equal or oftentimes surpass the younger martial artists.

We definitely were tougher back in the old days. We never wore any protective gear, and if you got hurt, other than very severe injuries, you kept on going. Much of the kumite training was to survive. It was that kind of dojo climate we all endured, and you had to be prepared for outsiders who would come to your dojo to basically challenge you (dojo yaburi).

The important point of my teaching is to utilize Karate-do as a vehicle to develop good character, healthy minds and bodies, and assist in directing those who I serve to learn to be of service to others. Students, on the other hand need, to understand and practice commitment. Students who are committed to learning correctly and training for the long haul provide me with the opportunity to expose them to all the necessary tools to build a solid foundation. From strong roots and with healthy spirits, students will be able to keep a healthy attitude to preserve the style for others to learn and enjoy.

I don't think that it is healthy or even reasonable to cling to things that have no room for improvement. Changes and adjustments are necessary as long as they don't wander too far from the original source. Can you imagine where medicine would be today if we kept it "pure" as of yesteryear?

Do you think different 'styles' are truly important in the art of Karate?
I think it is good to maintain the various styles, as each has many unique qualities and flavor. Styles offer healthy choices for students. Once they have come to understand their style, they can better appreciate other

styles while maintaining their unique characteristics and integrity.

What is your opinion of fighting events such as the UFC and Mixed Martial Arts?

I imagine there is a following for that type of fighting. Similar to the Gladiators fighting in the coliseum, the Roman emperor wanted the citizens to keep the warrior spirit alive as they were getting too passive. Perhaps there is a need for that way of thinking as these fights are gaining in popularity. Personally, I feel it should be kept away from the impressionable eyes of our youngsters.

Karate nowadays often is referred to as a sport. Would you agree with this definition, or is a martial art?

There is definitely "sport Karate." In fact, many athletes only practice kumite if they wish to excel in sparring, or practice only kata if they wish to perform well in that arena. True Karatekas learn how to defend themselves internally and externally. The delicate balance to practice correctly is definitely a part of the martial aspect of Karate. Senseis need to sculpt a landscape that all students, young and old, can appreciate. Too often, I see older students retire and put to pasture because the interests of their teachers have waned. A healthy dojo would have many seniors practicing eagerly for the love of the art, nothing more.

How do you think Karate has most influenced you?

By teaching me from a young age to be disciplined, focused, and balanced. By doing so, I became confident and overcame my shyness. What the public schools lacked in fulfilling my shortcomings, my Karate school provided. Throughout the years, Karate has opened the door to many opportunities to serve in a leadership capacity, such as serving as National Executive Director for the AAU Karate Program. Karate also has led me to meet many outstanding practitioners of the martial arts and has provided me the opportunity to help others overcome their obstacles. Karate has become a part of my life and, as life unfolds countless lessons, so does Karate. I am always searching for ways to keep students healthy and active, in order to provide me with enough time to teach them adequately.

As the new-age approach of teaching has invaded many circles, I want to maintain the disciplined dojo atmosphere without negative reactions from students or parents. Without the proper discipline and respect, teaching becomes almost a chore rather than a blessing.

When did you get involved with the AAU Karate?

In the mid-80s, I met Joe Mirza, a Shotokan practitioner, at one of Ray Dalke's tournaments in Riverside, California. Soon after that first meeting, Joe Mirza convinced me that I should become active in

---

the AAU National Karate Program, which he was chairman of. I guess he sensed that I was looking for an organization that I could really sink my teeth into, to make a difference in strengthening classical Karate-do in the U.S. He has accomplished many things in the sport arena that our earlier pioneers pursued but came up short on. His passion and dream to take Karate-do to greater heights of excellence also has made me partner with him to make that a reality.

How do you see Karate in the U.S. at the present time?

Confused. Instructors who have used martial arts as a business are winging the approaches of successful operators who make a hefty income from their dojos. I say more power to those who have been financially successful. I'm sure they are not losing any sleep at night, despite the fact that their students look rather sloppy in their techniques. Then you have those instructors who keep their students in one rank for a long time and boast how difficult it is to obtain a black belt at their school. Their classes are small and, even if their students look impressive, their growth potential is almost nil. How then can we keep Karate-do growing in a wholesome way without damaging the integrity of our precious treasure? All true senseis need to be finding a sane and wholesome solution.

How does the Karate style differ from other martial arts methods when applying the techniques in a self-defense situation?

I would hope that Karatekas would defend themselves wisely, quickly and effectively. By utilizing self-defense techniques of awareness, confidence, and positive body language, Karate students will be able to defend themselves before actually being attacked. Some of the other martial arts provoke one to attack just to test his or her abilities. I recall a martial art school in Hawaii that did just that. The instructor taught his students how to fight, and after training they would go to the local bar and stir up trouble with the GIs so they could test their techniques. Technically, Karate incorporates grappling, throwing, submission maneuvers, and non-tournament applications that are very effective. Regardless of the techniques applied, all martial arts methods, if executed correctly, can prove to be an effective means for self-defense.

Self-defense is a very important element in the art of Karate-do. And self-defense is not only physical but mental and emotional as well. Karate should be taught as a learning tool for competition. Life is competitive in many ways and one has to find the useful techniques to make the right choices to ward off all the attacks that they are confronted with.

Forms and sparring: what's the proper ratio in training?

In the beginning the ratio should be 90 percent kata. After the kihon is solid, sparring and forms should then be equal. Then, for those who reach the autumn of their lives, I feel the ratio to be 90 percent kata and a minimum percent spent on sparring. Kata is very important in the budo aspect of Karate-do. By practicing kata, one can fulfill physical and mental training and learn how to become victorious over oneself; that is, to destroy the enemy within. So many times, students, especially adults, are hesitant in performing kata in front of an audience due to their insecurities. Yet, by practice and encouragement, they learn to push that aside and come to enjoy the opportunity to share the movement of their body with the proper components with others. Kata also is a very ingenious way of transmitting information from teacher to student in order to preserve the style and self-defense techniques.

Do you have any general advice you would care to pass on to the practitioners?

Seek out the right sensei. One of the most important phases of training is the beginning. Correct application of techniques, healthy attitude, wholesome philosophy, and a clean and safe environment are important considerations to hold in your quest for Karate excellence.

Train regularly. Hold yourselves accountable to your trusted dojo mates and keep Karate a healthy attitude that nourishes your mind, body and spirit.

For senseis, learn to communicate effectively. It is an ongoing process that needs to be understood in depth in order for positive learning to take place. Instructors and students alike have a built-in bias in culture, religion, politics, and age. For example, in many circles, physical contact is taught to be kept within the immediate family. As a result, when a teacher corrects a student's technique by touching him or her, it may not be taken as the teacher intended, but rather cause a negative reaction because it may be in direct violation of the parent's rules. Religions that advocate that one should not bow to anyone but God bring questions of bowing to others in the dojo. And then there are those who teach their children to always question authority because many who are placed in superior positions have abused their power and taken advantage of those in their care. These are some of the filters that need to be addressed to maintain an open line of communication. Compared to the World War I veterans, who were totally committed to honor, respect, duty, and sacrifice, the baby boomers believe that honor is based on their personal ideals, duty is formulated with teamwork and not independent hard work, respect may come after authority is questioned, and respect is embraced only if it encompasses diversity.

What do you consider to be the major changes in the art since you began training?

More networking with other instructors and students is tolerated. The earlier pioneers were myopic and hard-headed in many ways and considered themselves to be the authorities of Karate-do, when, in reality, they were young, adjusting to a different culture, and building a reputation for themselves. They frowned upon mingling with practitioners of other styles not their own and made those who came from Japan achieve higher status no matter if they were juniors to those who were their senpai here in the States. This resulted in a major meltdown and the beginning of the American revolution of the martial arts. I don't know if we can bring the extreme right wing martial artist to some happy medium with the left, but those of us who understand Karate-do must work together to preserve what we have.

Who would you like to have trained with that you have not?

Chojun Miyagi and Kenwa Mabuni. Miyamoto Musashi for Iaijutsu. I would like to travel to Okinawa and spend a few months to train with the masters that have dedicated their lives to teaching and preserving their martial arts.

What can you tell us about the late Soke Mabuni Kenzo?

I came to know him as a dear friend, and I respected him greatly. He supported me when many of his own instructors, especially those in the United States, initially had doubts about me, especially when they were unclear as to my real motives in Karate-do. Soke Mabuni also recognized my organization as an important one for Karate-do. He made it possible for me to run my organization without having to interrupt our day-to-day operations by joining another organization. He provided me with a direct line to him. He trusted me with making wise decisions that would enhance the betterment of Shito-ryu in this country as well as abroad. When he stayed in my home, it was a treat to hear his stories of his dad and of what Karate meant to him. It was also a joy to go outside with him to practice kata. I was also very honored when Soke allowed me to organize the 4th International Shito Cup in Grants Pass. I admired him for being able to be a great leader, orchestrating, as well as challenging, all the leaders in his organization. I also saw the special joy he had seeing children performing kata. The smiles and twinkle in his eyes clearly told me what Karate is about. The autumn of his life began to wear on him; yet, although very frail, he managed to be a part of Karate events as often as he could. He loved Karate for the right reasons, and I will always remember that.

What keeps you motivated after all these years?

Students who have grown to be outstanding citizens and continue to be of service to others. Students who have overcome adversities thanks to their Karate training. My good friends and colleagues who continue to strive to maintain a sane and useful art. Students of Karate-do, young and old, such as Tony Mendonca, Ubiratan de Souza Lima, Joan Gombau, Amir Mahdavi, Tony Romano, Dwight Grover, Barbara and Robert Koncal, Rony Kluger, Tomohiro Arashiro, Charles Sweigeart, Jae Ferrell, Ray Irving, John Isabelo, John Limcaco, Basilio Bara, Francesco and Alessandra Arabi (to name a few) impress me with their Karate performance and sincerity. By their involvement, I know that Karate is in good hands and keep me motivated as well as hopeful.

I would add that you have made so many positive contributions that is necessary to preserve martial artist for many to enjoy for years to come, and appreciate all that you do.

What is the philosophical basis for your Karate training?

Train with what you are able to accomplish without injuring yourself. Always try your best but don't beat yourself down in the trying.

After all these years of training and experience, could you explain the meaning of the practice of Karate?

If you are talking about "keiko" (practice and training of the spirit) and not "renshuu" (training to learn something through repetition), I believe it goes hand-in-hand with "Shu-Ha-Ri" (the stages of learning and mastery). Drawing from the past to identify the core of Karate-do is important. Once a level of mastery is present, the journey then requires improvement to better the path of those who preceded us. Incorporate the infinite wisdom of old with modern concepts. This kind of understanding will keep the art improving with each generation. That is, and should be, the practice of Karate-do.

How do you think Karate practitioners can increase their understanding of the spiritual aspect of the art?

I believe that as one becomes more in harmony with oneself and with others, a deep spirited manifestation to seek truth becomes apparent. God has planted seeds in each one of us to grow and to seek Him. He has provided an internal compass to find Him. Through practice, one needs to understand what is God's will, as opposed to man's will. In the dojo, we are constantly appraised to determine our self-worth. Unlike buying a car or property, where the worth is based on the blue book or appraiser, our worth should not be left to the sole appraisal of the sensei. We need a higher source to keep our character value high. For example, there are instructors who keep students who make them look good on a pedestal and allow their shortcomings to be overlooked. Then there are those who will keep promoting students, not keeping them at a high standard, fearful that they may quit and reduce their financial bottom line. That self-interest equates to selfishness and ultimately results in disappointments. Senseis and students need to look for the interests of others. This will result in humility. Spiritually, then, we should all keep God as the captain of our ship and allow Him to direct us in our Karate mission in order that we may all stay the course.

Is anything lacking in the way martial arts are taught today compared to how they were you began?

I would have to say seriousness. We worked hard and learned karate to experience the unexpected. It was survival. If you were not serious, you paid for it. For many these days, Karate is just another seasonal extracurricular activity.

Could I ask you what you consider the most important qualities of a successful Karate practitioner?

Trustworthiness, humility, and sincerity, augmented with the willingness to train hard on a regular basis. Learning Karate-do to improve one's well-being and applying it in one's daily life in order to be a productive and outstanding citizen. To apply Karate lessons which have been rooted in one's moral values and overall conduct that defends one from negative peer pressures.

What advice would you give to students on the question of supplementary training (running, weights, etc.)?

I recommend wind sprints, correct methods of weight training, stretching, cross-training, plyometrics, and balancing these with healthy reading, fishing, karaoke, and golf.

Why do you think that a lot of students start falling away after two or three years of training?

I blame lack of enthusiasm, other extracurricular activities that fog the vision, classes that become boring and lack motivation. Also, there is an intrusion where difficult phases of their lives that need tending to. There is also lack of commitment; a disciplined environment (like the dojo) is not readily accepted by today's youth. Other activities such as soccer, computer games, parents who don't take the time to teach their children commitment, and an ever-present relaxed overall attitude that conflicts with the structured and disciplined dojo environment.

And, in addition, the old methods of teaching Karate needs to be modified in order to keep students long enough to be able to teach them the true benefits of Karate-do. Instructors need to reevaluate their teaching methods in order to maintain a good student enrollment. There are many fun extra-curricular activities that can enhance enrollment. In this day and age, many technically unqualified Karate instructors, (as judged by the traditional masters), pack their schools with hundreds of students because their modern methods of teaching fit in perfectly with the times, and their impressive marketing and business savvy, puts many masters to shame.

For other disciplines, one questionable marketing strategy is to make the rank of black belt easily attainable, much easier than at classical dojos. Once achieved, this new black belt elevates their status and spreads the "notoriety'" of their style, school and instructor. Traditional instructors, on the other hand, relish how hard it is for their students to achieve the black belt. The differences between the two schools become a "no-brainer" when a parent asks how many students have achieved their black belt this year, and you say, "5," compared to that 100 that were awarded in a non-traditional school. I'm not advocating that we all begin teaching that way or begin handing out black belts, but we certainly need to re-think how we can preserve our art.

What led you to become the Director for the Traditional Karate-do Federation International?

I would have to say that all the interesting chapters of my life led to my present position with the TKFI. In the late 60s, Al Kahalekulu retired completely from Karate. He gave me the authority to continue teaching Chitose-ryu and promoted me to Godan. I then formed the Goshinjutsu Organization and was unattached to any other organization at that time. My dad had heard the name Goshinjutsu and said that it was a good name so I agreed. I had Kahalekulu sensei sign each certificate and operated the independent organization until the early 70s, when I joined Chuzo Kotaka's IKF. Kotaka sensei had made a few changes in his organizational operations, which led to my resignation from the IKF. I informed all of my branch instructors of my decision and gave them my blessing if they wished to remain attached with the IKF. Fortunately for me, they all decided to trailblaze with me.

In 2009, after Kenzo Mabuni Soke gave me his blessings to continue my Karate journey on my own, and without any constraint from his organization, I decided to organize the Traditional Karate-do Federation International. As you may know, this gesture of trust and goodwill is almost unheard of. In fact I am the only instructor that Soke has ever allowed to remain independent. Discussing my plans with my trusted instructors, they all agreed that it was a perfect time to launch TKFI. This organization was to primarily preserve Shito-ryu Karate-do and to provide other Shito-ryu instructors a home for higher learning without dealing with politics and financial burdens. So after launching ceremonies in Italy, New York, Brazil, Hawaii and Oregon, the TKFI was born.

What leadership roles do you presently have or have had?

I presently am the owner and operator of Del Saito's Martial Arts Training Center, president of the International Karate-do Federation International, and Vice President and Technical Director for the World Traditional Okinawan Karate Federation which is headed by Leone Bara.

During my ten plus years with the Amateur Athletic Program, I served as a member of the AAU Board of Directors, the Executive Director for the AAU National Karate Program, Director of AAU Karate Regional 12, Chairman of Oregon AAU Karate, and Governor of Oregon AAU for all sports.

For my community in Grants Pass, I served as President of the Grants Pass Asian Cultural Society, board member of the YMCA, and past Vice-President for Crime Stoppers of Josephine County.

What would be your ideal for Karate in the USA?

That Karate would be incorporated into every junior and high school. I think there is a definite need in the school system for this kind of training, which could benefit everyone involved. I believe that ingredients of discipline, respect, honor, awareness, motivation, accountability, responsibility, and community service provided in a dojo atmosphere would definitely extend into the classroom. I see so many good kids who have too much unsupervised - time that gets them in trouble. If we could only figure out a way to minimize that problem and get them involved in a wholesome yearly activity, the lessons they would reap will keep them from learning the hard way.

To what do you attribute the success of your program?

Honesty, fairness, and my autocratic methods of running my program have been the keys to the success of our schools and organization. Karate sensei, students, and parents need to be assured that what we provide is a sound program that will be of benefit to them. I always make sure that each person has ample time to research our program before admitting him or her to our school or organization. I go over what is expected of them and what they can expect from me. My leadership in the dojo is not democratic because, throughout all the years of teaching, I have found it to be ineffectual, that it leads to wasted time, confusion, and at times even corruption. Those who understand what our service provides for them will stay and become a vital force in keeping the positive training spirit alive. Those who choose not to embrace our philosophy will fade away and not harm the prestige or integrity of our program. As for training, I still demand the utmost respect and discipline from every student. They do not leave the mat as they wish, and I expect them to give their best effort. Their achievements are based on their own hard work and diligence, and once they figure that out, they have learned the formula for success. I also end each class with a brief discussion on lessons of life, which include nutrition, be-havior, community service, and drugs, to name a few.

Success also goes hand-in-hand with my staff, which I am forever grateful. I have dedicated instructors who share their time and knowledge with all of our members. The gals that run the front office keeps everything organized, including me.

Who do you think are the top Karate athletes these days?

The notables in the United States are Sakura Kokumai, Shannon Nishi, Jessica Kwong, Madeline Kenneway, Ariel Torres, Tozaki Gakuji, Mason Stiwell, Brandon Arashiro, Tom Scott, Eduard Sagilyan, and Trinity Allen. I've enjoyed watching these athletes mature not only in the competition arena but in life as well. They are awesome technicians and skilled in martial arts, and most of all, they are well-mannered, respectful, and great role models.

Do you think that Olympics will be positive for the art of Karate-do in case that happens one day?

I don't know about the art of Karate, but it may be for the sport if it maintains many of the classical principles that we now embrace. If the in-ternational sports leaders constantly change the composition of Karate just to satisfy the sport aspect, then the UFC type of fighting may seem to be more appropriate for the International Olympic Committee. It would cer-tainly be clearer who the winners are.

Personally, I would push for Kata and oyo/bunkai for the Olympics. I think it would be a much easier sell to the IOC. Once established, kumite may find an easier path for acceptance.

What are your thoughts on the future of Karate?

I am very optimistic. Although many of the pioneers of Karate in this country had their shortcomings, those who made a sincere attempt to teach and preserve what they knew with passion and conviction can be appreciated and respected for their efforts. Likewise, today's instructors must teach wholesomely and seize every opportunity to keep Karate-do from eroding, and to maintain its integrity for future generations to enjoy.

Karate-do in Iran unites us with understanding, compassion, vision and common sense.

Women in Iran train with their hijab symbolizing religious commitment and devotion, but does not distract them from their karate training.

APPENDIX
KARATE TERMINOLOGY

The following karate terms have been included to give you a more thorough understanding of and professional outlook on Karate-do. Memorize a few each day, saying each term out loud. You might wish to put the terms on cards to carry with you for easy practice.

VOWEL SOUNDS IN JAPANESE
A= ah
E= ay
I= ee
O=oh
U=oo

GENERAL TERMS

Karate	empty hand
Karate-do	way of karate
Karate-ka	karate student
Dojo	training gym
Gi	uniform
Obi	belt
Sensei	teacher
Senpai	senior student
Kohai	junior student
Rei	bow
Shomen ni	to front
Otagai ni	to each other
Sensei ni	to teacher
Kata	formal exercise "form" or "shape"
Kime	focus
Waza	technique
Osu	karate greeting
Hai	yes
Ie	no
Wakarimasu	understand
Hajime	begin
Yame	stop
Yoi	ready
Kamaete	assume position
Kiai	spirit shout
Arrigato gozaimashita	thank you very much
Oneigaishimasu	please let's train hard

Mae	front
Ushiro	back
Hidari	left
Migi	right
Mawate	turn around
Renshu	training of the body
Keiko	practice or training of the spirit
Keage	snap
Kekomi	thrust
Nage-waza	throwing technique
Ma-ai	distancing
Makiwara	punching board
Jodan	face area
Chudan	chest area
Gedan	lower area of body
Suki	opening

DACHI (stance)

Musubi-dachi	informal attention stance, feet turned out
Heisoku-dachi	informal attention stance, feet together
Zenkutsu-dachi	forward stance
Neko-ashi-dach	cat stance
Kiba-dachi	horse stance
Kokutsu-dachi	back stance
Shiko-dachi	square stance
Uchi-hachiji-dachi	inverted open-leg stance
Sanchin-dachi	hourglass stance
Kosa-dachi	cross-leg stance
Renoji-dachi	L-stance
Heiko-dachi	parallel stance
Sagiashi-dachi	one-leg stance

STRIKING PARTS OF LEG AND FOOT

Koshi	ball of foot
Kakato	heel
Sokuto	edge of foot
Hittsui	knee
Haisoku	instep
Teisoku	sole or bottom of foot

STRIKING PARTS OF ARMS AND HANDS

Seiken	forefist
Riken	backfist
Tettsui	bottom fist
Ippon-ken	one-knuckle fist
Hiraken	fore-knuckle fist
Haito	ridge hand
Haishu	back hand
Kumade	bear hand
Nukite	spear hand
Nihon nukite	two-finger spear hand
Shuto	knife hand
Ude	forearm
Kakuto	bent wrist
Teisho	palm heel
Seiryuto	ox-jaw hand
Empi (hiji)	elbow

UKE WAZA (blocking techniques)

Jodan-age-uke	high-rising block
Soto-uke	outward block
Naka-uke	inward block
Gedan-barai	downward block
Shuto-uke	knife-hand block
Morote-uke	supporting elbow block
Juji-uke	X block
Kakiwake-uke	wedge block
Tsukami-uke	grasping block
Nagashi-uke	sweeping block
Osae-uke	press block
Suki-uke	scooping block

KERI WAZA (kicking techniques)

Mae-geri	front kick
Yoko-geri	side kick
Mawashi-geri	roundhouse kick
Ushiro-geri	back kick
Mika-zuki-geri	crescent kick
Fumikomi	stamping kick
Mae-tobi-geri	flying front kick
Yoko-tobi-geri	flying side kick
Hittsui-geri	knee kick

TSUKI WAZA (thrusting techniques)

Seiken-choku-zuki	forefist straight punch
Gyaku-zuki	reverse punch
Oi-zuki	lunge thrust
Tate-zuki	vertical punch
Age-zuki	rising punch
Mawashi-zuki	round punch
Morote-zuki	double-fist punch
Ura-zuki	uppercut punch
Kagi-zuki	hook punch
Kizami-zuki	jab

KUMITE (sparring)

Kihon kumite	basic sparring
Ippon kumite	one-strike sparring
Sanbon kumite	three-strike sparring
Jyu-ippon kumite	semi-free one strike sparring
Jyu kumite	free-style sparring

TOURNAMENT TERMS

Shobu	match or bout
Hajime	begin
Yame	temporary stop
Tsuzukete hajime	reopening
Jogai nakae	return to match area
Motonoichi	return to fixed positions
Jikan	timekeeper to keep time
Yuko	one point
Waza-ari	two points
Ippon	three points
Yame soremade	end of match
Aka no kachi	victory of red
Ao no kachi	victory of blue
Hantei	judgment
Hansoku	foul
Hansoku chui	warning of a foul
Atoshibaraku	a little time remaining
Fukushin shugo	calling together the judges
Kiken	renunciation
Torimasen	unacceptable as a scoring technique
Yowai	weak
Maai	poor distance of the technique
Jogai	out of bounds
Shikakau	disqualification

GREETINGS

Ohio gozaimasu	"Good Morning"
Konichiwa	"Good Afternoon" or "Good Day"
Komban wa	"Good Evening"
Sayonara	"Goodbye"

NUMBERS

Rei	zero
Ichi	one
Ni	two
San	three
Shi	four
Go	five
Roku	six
Shichi	seven
Hachi	eight
Ku	nine
Ju	ten
Juu-ichi	eleven
Ni-ju	twenty
San-ju	thirty
Yon-ju	forty
Go-ju	fifty
Roku-ju	sixty
Nana-ju	seventy
Hachi-ju	eighty
Kyuu-ju	ninety
Hyaku	one hundred

A SAMPLING OF KOBUDO WEAPONS KATAS

BO (Staff)
> Sakugawa no kon
> Shiu-shi no kon
> Chanton yara no kon
> Aragaki no kon
> Ko Bo
> Rohai no kon
> Sueyoshi no kon
> Ko-ryu Bo
> Katin no kun

TONFA
> Hamahiga no tonfa

SAI (Short Swords)
> Tsuken shitahaku no sai
> Chanton-yara no sai
> Towada no sai
> Aragaki no sai
> Hamahiga no sai

EKU
> Ten no kata
> Chi no kata
> Futen no kata

NIUNCHAKU
> Nunchaku kata Sho

PRINCIPLES AND RULES

All members shall memorize and practice the following principles at all times.

1. Henceforth, I shall faithfully train to strengthen my mind and body.
2. I am willing to endure rigorous training to achieve my goal.
3. As my strength increases, I shall seek to cultivate a gentle heart.
4. I shall not use my skill outside the dojo except in the most extreme circumstances.
5. At all times I will try to avoid inflicting injury upon another person.
6. I will not brag about my skill nor use it maliciously.
7. I shall train with the spirit of humility.

Other rules of conduct shall include the following:

1. Vulgar language is never allowed either inside or outside the dojo.
2. Smoking is prohibited in the dojo at all times.
3. Alcoholic beverages are never allowed in the dojo.
4. Unprescribed or mind-altering drugs are strictly forbidden at all times.
5. The karate gi should be kept clean and in good repair at all times. Unauthorized patches of any kind shall not be allowed on the gi.
6. All students are asked to keep their fingernails and toenails carefully clipped. Jewelry should not be worn.
7. A dignified appearance is always proper and will reflect on the reputation toward our organization.
8. Once the practice session begins, no one is to break ranks unless given permission to do so.
9. Students should be ready to start training at the designated starting time. Any student arriving late is to meditate and warm up briefly before joining the ranks with the least disturbance to the class.
10. Do not speak ill of others, including other martial arts instructors, students, and others. "The mountain does not laugh at the river because it is lowly, nor does the river speak ill of the mountain because it cannot move."
11. No street shoes are allowed on main dojo floor. If shoes have been worn all day prior to entering dojo, please wash your feet.
12. Leave your food, chewing gum, etc. at home.
13. Injuries or illness must be reported to your instructor at once.
14. Improper behavior or violation of club rules can result in termination of karate class and membership.

BY-LAWS
AND RESOLUTIONS

I WILL:
1. Never use my hands and feet without a just cause.
2. Never accept nor challenge anyone to duel.
3. Never criticize other clubs or its members.
4. Never speak ill of the absent.
5. Respect the rights of others at all times.
6. Develop tolerance through the knowledge of these arts.
7. Avoid all arguments.
8. Curb my impetuousness and think before acting.
9. Be extremely hesitant in using any of these dangerous techniques even in my own defense.
10. Participate in all class projects.
11. Practice these arts patiently, diligently, and in the proper state of mind.
12. Be honest, humble, courteous, and sincere at all times.
13. Never carry a chip on my shoulder.
14. Always strive for spiritual, mental, and physical strength.
15. Never hurt my fellow students during practice.
16. Avoid all pettiness.
17. Forgive the ignorant and practice self-control at all times.
18. Never boast or use profane language.
19. Treasure these arts and never display them needlessly.

RESOLUTIONS:
1. Never invite trouble through uncalled-for looks, remarks, or actions.
2. Make every effort to smile or talk, and not fight my way out of trivial situations.
3. Never become involved with the domestic quarrels of my neighbors.
4. Ignore the rantings of a rowdy, belligerent person, drunk or otherwise.
5. Never start a fight with a weaker person just to assert my physical superiority.
6. Steer clear of all trouble-prone areas or walk away from such places at the first sign of trouble.

SAMPLE LIST OF KATA

Kihon Kata
Pinan Shodan to Godan
Jyuroku
Jiin
Jitte
Jion
Sanchin
Bassai Sho
Bassai Dai
Tomari Bassai
Matsumura Bassai
Aoyagi
Rohai Shodan to Sandan
Matsukaze
Wanshu
Kosoku Sho
Kosokun Dai
Shiho Kosoku
Chantanyara Kushanku
Naihanchin Shodan to Sandan
Tensho
Saifa
Seisan
Seienchin
Sanseiryu
Seipai
Kururunfa
Chintei
Chinto
Gojushiho
Nijyushiho
Annanko
Unshu
Suparimpei

Paiku
Pachu
Anan
Heiku
Nipaipo
Papuren

BASIC MEANING OF KATAS

Kihon	Basic
Pinan	Peaceful
Jyuroku	16
Jiin	Temple ground
Jion	Temple sound
Jiite	Temple hand (10 hands)
Bassai	To penetrate a fortress
Aoyagi	Green willow
Rohai	Vision of white heron
Matsukaze	Pine tree wind
Wanshu	Excellent wrist
Kosokun	Named after a Chinese diplomatic official
Naihanchin	Fighting on home ground or Sideways fighting
Tensyo	Change of hands
Sanchin	3 Battles
Saiha	Final breaking point
Sochin	Grand prize or Fighting old man
Shisochin	Fighting 4 monks or 19
Seisan	13
Seippai	18 cupfuls
Seienchin	The Lull in the storm
Sanseiryu	36
Kururunha	Come stay waves, also To restrain and destroy.
Chintei	Winning hand
Chinto	Fighting to the east
Gojyushiho	54 steps
Nijyushiho	24 steps
Annanko	Light from the south
Unsyu	Hand in the clouds
Suparimpei	108
Papuren	8 steps at the same time
Pachu	To twirl a ball
Paiku	White tiger
Heiku	Black tiger

REFLECTIONS

Karate training at Shuri Castle.

Seminar presented by Kenzo Mabuni Soke in Grants Pass, Oregon.

Eager students always looking forward to a good training session in Tiruppur, in the Indian state of Tamil Nadu.

Tony Mendonca Kyoshi having a great time teaching students with one of our affiliates in India.

Students in India seem to be more focused on karate training, compared to other students in the United States who are much more privileged.

Wonderful experience training with the many students in Southern India, under the directorship of Gowtham Ragunathan, who is following his father Kaysavan's foot-steps.

At our yearly gasshuku in Switzerland, with the assistance of Joan Gombau.

Fond memories of the times spent with Kenzo Mabuni soke.

Serious students from Europe gather to train together in Romania, and always give their best effort.

Families who train together, stay together, as these students demonstrate at our Hawaii branch.

Special moments spent with Kenzo Mabuni soke, my teacher and friend,

Kenzo Mabuni with my dad Toshio.

Enjoying a nice day at Osaka Castle.

Instructors always willing to assist in promoting the Asian culture.

A unique venue to host the Saito Karate-do Classic at the Evergreen Space and Aviation Museum in McMinnville, Oregon. Organized and directed by Tony Mendonca, this annual event continues to be very successful.

Educating students about the benefits of Karate at a Grants Pass charter school.

Teaching STEM (science, technology, engineering, and mathematics) students, at the Rogue Community College, the benefits of Karate.

Sharing the benefits of Karate to the staff at Options for Southern Oregon, an agency that serves people of all ages in our community with mental health and addiction treatment needs.

Karate masters whose mission is to preserve the true art of karate-do. (l-r) James Miyaji, the author, Lim Sison, Kenzo Mabuni, Minobu Miki, and Masayuki Shima-bukuro.

Volunteers serve the needs of the community at the annual "Girls Rock" event (which provides fun-filled classes for girls ages 9-13), who with their parents or another adult, participate in activities that foster communication and explore the fields of science, engineering, math, technology, and Karate-do.

The Brazil Karate-do Union shows once again that the essence of Karate-do is not just punches and kicks, and that not all victories are on top of the tatami. The Karate-Do Angels Program, created by Kyoshi Ubiratan de Souza Lima (a Shihan Kai member), aims to encourage children and adolescents of the project to always help and stand in solidarity with those most in need.

Kazumasa Itaki sensei's special tournament, outside of Tokyo, brings joy to all participants.

Dedicated Karate masters tirelessly working to preserve the future of Karate. Front row (l-r) Chuck Merriman, Fumio Demura, Kenzo Mabuni, and Chuzo Kotaka. Back row (l-r) Rony Kluger, Joe Mirza, and the author.

World Karate Federation President Antonio Espinos and other Karate leaders meeting in Los Angeles in hopes that Karate be included in the 2028 Summer Olympics.

Practicing in winter months provide students mental toughness.

After running for an hour, students do a hundred blocks and kicks.

Followed by a hundred thrusting techniques in the cold and rain.

Returning to the dojo, students then endure a vigorous circuit training workout.

Grimacing and pushing themselves to their limits provides mental and physical toughness.

Ending the three-hour training with kata practice. Now they can face life's challenges with a positive attitude.

Hawaii instructors from various styles training together..

Filming of Marshall Martial with Nori Bunasawa.

A "Martial Arts Sheriff" - not a bad idea for many cities.

Long hours getting the fight scenes just right.

Director Bob Clouse, who also directed "Enter the Dragon."

Shin Koyamada, with wife Nia, has been appointed as WKF Karate Ambassador. Shin is the co-founder of KIF (Koyamada International Foundation), and is the President of Chime TV International, a national Asian American TV cable network and digital platform in the United States.

Koyamada is also known for his philanthropic efforts in youth leadership, humanitarian aid, gender equality, citizen diplomacy, climate action, and habitat conservation.

SAITO-HA SHITO-RYU KARATE-DO
FOR THE MODERN WARRIOR
齋藤派糸東流空手道

SAITO-HA SHITO-RYU KARATE-DO
FOR THE MODERN WARRIOR

This book captures the very essence of the true principles taught by Sensei Del Saito to many students here in the United States and abroad. Over many decades of teaching experience, he focuses on the development of good character, a healthy mind and body, and the higher calling for serving others. This work is an especially good read for parents who want to instill in their children, good moral character, confidence, discipline, and leadership skills. The inception of this book began in the 1980s when the author decided to collect all his notes, thoughts, and experiences together and present them in an organized book. The knowledge set forth in this book will share with you, the student of Karate, information he attained in his lifelong passion of devotion to martial arts.

In 2008, at the age of sixty, he decided to explore a new avenue in his study of Karate. He was drawn to the artistic and powerful pure Shito-ryu style and began training with the Nihon Karate-do Kai under Master Kenzo Mabuni, son of Kenwa Mabuni, founder of the Shito-ryu style. Soke Mabuni was so impressed with his Karate-do knowledge and organizational skills that he gave Del his blessing for to pursue his personal vision of Shito-ryu independently, without the constraint of any organization. Del Saito is the only instructor granted this high honor by Kenzo Mabuni Soke.

The foundation of Del Saito's teaching is preserving and teaching the true essence of Karate while instilling a sense of human decency in his students.

Now available in paperback at Amazon.com for $29.95 USD

With Brendal, a 450 pound Bengal tiger.

Passage is also a Bengal tiger. He knows instinctively the exact point to attack, and the force with which he attacks will break the spine of its prey. Training with Passage keeps us totally aware and focused, and strengthens our fighting spirit.

9 781949 753561

9 781949 753561